Survival Kit
for Leaders

John C. Kunich, J. D.

Richard Lester, Ph.D.

Skyward Publishing
Dallas, Texas

Copyright © 2003 by Skyward Publishing, Inc.

Publisher: Skyward Publishing, Inc.
              Dallas, Texas
              E-Mail: info@skywardpublishing.com
              Website: www.skywardpublishing.com

Library of Congress Cataloging-Publication Data

Kunich, John C. 1953-
    Survival Kit for Leaders / John C. Kunich and Richard I.
    Lester.p. cm.
    Includes bibliographical references.
    ISBN 1-881554-25-2
    1. Leadership. I. Lester, Richard I, II. Title
    2nd Print

HD57.7.K858 2002
658.4'092–dc21   2003070496

TABLE OF CONTENTS

Chapters

FOREWORD
by
KEN BLANCHARD

Are you wondering why the world needs–or why you need–one more book on leadership? There are already books that tell you how to emulate Attila the Hun, how to use seven habits to become highly effective, and even–ahem–how to be a one-minute manager. So why should you read *Survival Kit for Leaders?*

The key is this book's power to teach and to reach, not just to preach, not just to occupy more space on your over-flowing library shelves. Dr. Lester and Professor Kunich have made their careers as both real-world leaders and as success-ful teachers. They know how to teach. They know what makes for effective teaching and what does not. They possess the educational secrets that spell the difference between sparking their learners' interest and lullabying them to sleep. They have spent many years in the pedagogical trenches, developing tech-niques that get through hard skulls and layers of apathy to penetrate and stimulate the human brain, that most impreg-nable of all fortresses.

From law school to Sunday school, from military gradu-ate schools to international seminars, these authors have learned what it takes to teach and have taught so that others can learn. They have loaded *Survival Kit for Leaders* with pow-erful methods not found in any other leadership and management book known to me. There are certainly other books that discuss time management and mentoring techniques, how to motivate people, and how to set and achieve goals—but this is the first and only book to teach these and other key principles with an interactive, memory-enhancing, life-relating approach.

A significant component of leadership is teaching, and good teachers know that people learn much more when they are actively involved. Subliminal messages and learning-while-sleeping techniques are no match for a mind that is fully awake and engaged in vigorous give and take with other minds. When we think, critically evaluate, compare, consider alternatives, relate principles to our own experiences, and apply the good examples of others to our own situations, we do more than read. We learn, we grow, and we transform. *Survival Kit for Leaders* is the result of Dr. Lester's and Professor Kunich's expert application of teaching mastery to leadership.

I am convinced that if you will use the thought-provoking questions at the end of every chapter of this book—really use them—this will be more than just another book for you. It will become your teacher. It will jolt your mind out of its autopilot doldrums and make it massage the messages in this book. You will actively and interactively transport yourself into new territories, identifying with great leaders and thinking about how your challenges are both unique and similar to those that have stood before other leaders. This book, properly used, is a true learning experience, individually tailored to the particular needs of every person who reads it. It is a custom-designed survival kit, made to order for you.

One strange thing about leadership is that many of us wrongly assume we are not leaders and have no need for leadership skills. This is a major cause of problems in the world today. The truth is, all of us are leaders.

Leaders are not only those "in charge" of formal organizations in the realm of government or business. True, when we think "leader" we often think first of presidents, members of Congress, governors, mayors, military officers, and CEOs and their counterparts at all levels of managerial responsibility in business organizations. But anyone who is a parent is also a leader of the children in his or her family–and there is no more vital leadership responsibility than in the home. Mothers and fathers are the leaders who most directly shape the future of the world, one child at a time. We are also leaders within our families on other levels, in the same generation (with our siblings and cousins), and with our relatives from both older and younger generations, as we help our loved ones work through difficulties large and small. Too, many of us serve in volunteer organizations, including religious groups, helping, service-oriented enterprises, and a host of other non-profit activities that do so much of the heavy lifting in human society.

The fact is that we are all leaders and followers. *Survival Kit for Leaders* has the power to change lives. Read it, use it, work with it, and apply it. You will be amazed at the results.

Dedication

I dedicate this book to my dear wife, Marcia K. Vigil, and to our wonderful daughters, Christina Laurel Kunich and Julie-Kate Marva Kunich, in loving gratitude for the light they have shone into my life and to Marva Collins, the greatest teacher, mentor, and leader I have ever known.

John Kunich

To the men and women of our Armed Forces whose courage and valor contribute immeasurably to the defense of our country and our way of life.

Richard Lester

Preface

How does a leader become—and stay—a survivor? Not just by buying this book, although we certainly thank you for doing that. But, sad to say, leadership simply is not that simple.

If you are like us, you already own dozens, even hundreds, of books you have never read. These books decorate your bookshelves like props on a Hollywood set—intellectual window-dressing—or fill boxes tucked away in your closets and basement. They provide weighty ballast to hold your house down when high winds threaten to carry it to Oz. They give you something to dust. But, unread books do not turn us into good leaders.

Well, what if you take the bold additional step of actually reading this book? Will that ensure your survival in the untamed world of leadership? As the saying goes, "It couldn't hurt." But most of us have read plenty of books and, much of the time, 20 minutes later, our brains are hungry again. The words we read go in one eye and out the other. Nothing sticks in our mind—we scarcely remember we ever read the books at all. A no-stick feature might be desirable for a frying pan but not for a book. Passive auto-pilot reading might be relaxing, even sleep-inducing, and it might impress people watching you studiously engaged in the act of reading, but it does not carry you into the realm of leadership.

We wrote *Survival Kit for Leaders* to overcome these twin tendencies for books to go smoothly and swiftly from purchase to landfill while making zero impact on our lives. We want this book to transform you. We have built in some key tools that can make this happen–if you use them.

First, we have included several discussion questions at the end of each chapter. Please read these questions *before* you read each chapter, so you will have them in mind. Then, after you finish reading a chapter, read the questions *again*, one at a time. But more than that–STOP and THINK about how you would answer every question before going on to the next one.

If you are using this book as a text in a course, actively discuss possible answers to each question with your fellow students. Hear the other students out. Listen and learn as well as speak. If you are not in a classroom situation, try to find at least two or three other people who can also read the chapter and then discuss the questions with them. If you can, pick some people who usually look at things differently from you–folks with whom you often disagree. This will ensure that you will benefit from a diversity of viewpoints that will help you to consider multiple aspects of every issue, evaluate them in depth, and arrive at your own mature, informed judgment on each point. If other people are not available, at least brainstorm and write down several plausible alternative ways of answering every question. Then list some pros and cons of each, on paper, and decide on your own optimal answer.

This process of developing, analyzing, and evaluating answers to each of the questions will enormously increase the benefits you derive from *Survival Kit for Leaders*. You will *think*, actively and interactively, about the material in each chapter. You will remember much more of what you read, and, more importantly, you will make it your own. You will *apply* the principles to your own life, your own experiences, and your own circumstances, and make them real and practical for you, individually. This is absolutely essential. If you are unwilling to think about the questions after each chapter, please do *not* buy our book. It will be a waste of money and will do you no good. We do not want your money under these circumstances.

In addition to the discussion questions, we have included mnemonics in some of the chapters to aid you further in recalling the main points. In some of the chapters where we identify multiple key points, we have organized these points into an acronym or acrostic so that the first letter of each point spells out the subject of the chapter. Check out the chapters on FEEDBACK and MENTORING to see what we mean. By using these mnemonics, you will have another tool to use in retaining the main aspects of what you have read. You will have them available, ready to use, whenever you need them, even on those rare and desperate occasions when you do not have a copy of *Survival Kit for Leaders* at your fingertips.

Finally, we have loaded each chapter with real-world examples of outstanding leaders. Their stories are inspiring. They illustrate the best and highest of human potential. When you think about the leadership skills of heroes such as Jackie Robinson, Anne Sullivan, Marva Collins, Raoul Wallenberg, and many other great people, it is hard not to be moved and moved not only emotionally but also moved in the sense of becoming *motivated* to be better than we are. These stellar examples can help you to muster the resolve to make the most of your life and the opportunities every day of life sends you. Then, the other tools in this survival kit will be more capable of making you into a more effective, more inspirational leader.

In short, this is an *interactive* book. It contains survival tools that will enable you to learn, to recall, and to apply powerful leadership principles directly and effectively in your own life. If you use this book with this in mind, it will make a real difference for you. You will survive your leadership challenges, and more–you will transcend them.

John C. Kunich
Richard I. Lester

> *"Leadership is the act of accomplishing more than the science of management says is possible."*
>
> General Colin Powell

Chapter 1

Leadership for a Survival Organization

Executive Summary

This chapter sets forth a framework for leadership within the context of a survival organization and paves the way for the more substantive chapters of this book. It establishes the premise that leadership is an essential element in achieving organizational effectiveness and durability. The focus of this discussion is a statement of principles, illustrated by concepts, providing a frame of reference for developing leadership skills to heighten administrative and functional endurance. The intent is to give an overview of the anatomy and demonstrated importance of leadership in achieving organizational longevity. There can be no significant institutional excellence without leadership. Organizations in the process of implementing value-added, constructive changes within today's highly competitive international environment will immediately recognize the importance of leadership at every organizational level to sustain constancy. This chapter and those that follow are intended to provide survival leaders with the guidance they need to make intelligent, informed leadership decisions to help them win in the leadership game.

Discussion

Leadership for Survivors

In the study of survival leadership, you just can't look under the hood. You must be able to take the engine apart and examine how it works. This book is an attempt to do just that. What kind of leadership is appropriate for today's survival organization? And just what is survival leadership? On balance, there are two kinds of people in organizations: the movers and shakers and those who are moved and shaken. Quality leaders are of the first kind. They are obviously committed: they believe their organizations can and will achieve more and better success under their leadership—organizational persistence does count. Leaders make things happen, challenge the status quo, and shake things up. Survival leaders assuredly know beforehand that at the crossroads of change stand 10,000 guardians of the past stationed behind barriers of inertia; however, they also know how to go over, around, and through these impending obstacles. Their goal is relentless pursuit of constructive, value-added change. Survival leaders do not ask, "What do I want?" They ask, "What needs to be done?" Then they ask, "What can and should I do to make a difference?"

Survivor leaders offer a simple, fluent appeal to continuous improvement. Leaders inspire people to continue the race, even though there is no apparent finish line. The most effective leaders are great simplifiers who have the capacity to defuse argument, cut prolonged debate, ease doubt, and offer realistic solutions to which people can relate and embrace. In pursuing excellence, these leaders focus on defining goals in simple terms so people in all echelons can believe that mutual goals are important and attainable. These leaders also have distinct personal images, which communicate the ability to project a firm commitment toward sustained progress.

A survival organization must offer hope and positive change; therefore, leadership must ensure an organization's climate does not chill or turn energy into disillusioned despair. Although leaders set the direction, achievement of momentum in progressive organizations must be built and persistently measured by individuals–at all levels–who believe they can unite around a philosophy and practice designed to make a good organization even better. What is needed today is a heightened moral commitment to bring about value-added changes to carry organizations through the twenty-first century and beyond.

Empowerment, Not Power

Leadership is not so much concerned with power as it is with empowerment. Steadfast leaders understand that the extent to which they empower their work force largely determines how well they succeed. The empowerment concept is deeply rooted in leadership theory and practice because, at their core, people want to make a difference. They want to have more control over those things for which they are responsible. Warren Bennis is right, "Empowerment is the collective effect of leadership." Leadership emphasizes building balanced work teams of responsible players who effectively work together. Survival leaders encourage their people to support each other and share a "can-do" collective pattern of positive behavior. This type of leadership promotes individual worth, initiative, and independence while simultaneously building cohesive and focused teams to enhance unit performance.

It usually consists of three distinct subsystems—namely, customer focus, employee involvement, and continuous improvement. To achieve this, it is essential that leaders have a deep commitment to vision, the humility to admit they do not have all the answers, and the willingness to learn and adapt as circumstances evolve.

As the central figures in any productive effort, leaders must measure success by their ability to motivate, support, train, give constructive feedback, and ultimately reward performance. Effective leaders directly influence their people to achieve value-added excellence. The best leaders understand that leadership is the liberation of talent. Our observations of top business executives suggest that survival leaders foster methods to obtain exceptional performance by involving average people in above-average ways. They focus on how to reenergize people—or, all too often, to energize and inspire them for the first time in their adult lives—so as to ignite the kind of fire and enthusiasm that enables productivity to flourish. They trust their instincts and impulses and are goal oriented.

Syndicated Leadership

Great leaders syndicate, or share, leadership throughout an organization. They communicate, set clear goals, define objectives, and ensure all organizational levels understand these goals and objectives. They put the right people in the right job—doing the right things for the right reasons. They teach each person to develop the same process in their respective work areas and thus spread purposeful leadership throughout the system. Leaders serve as mentors and positive role models during this entire procedure by being active, staying in touch, learning from mistakes, having a basic value system, knowing how to communicate clearly, knowing their job as well as knowing their boss' job, and making it easier for the boss to accomplish the mission—and, in the process, "having fun." This book, beginning in Chapter 3, shows in detail how to achieve all of these things.

These leadership practices help to promote organizational as well as personal success. The results are empowered people, rewards for the achievements of collective teams, not only individuals, improved multi-way communications, and abiding commitment to continuous positive change from all parts of the organization. In accomplishing these results, effective leaders influence others not by ordering them to do something, but by causing them to want to attempt it, not by telling people what to do, but by explaining why something is important. Survival leaders have the unique capacity to communicate and share a compelling vision, one others will want to make happen. Knowledge alone cannot cause these things to occur. If it could, librarians and professors would rule the world. Knowledgeable leaders must couple technical expertise with credibility and trustworthiness. These are key factors in subordinates' judgment of an effective leader. Good leaders do not send out "I do not trust you" messages. People who believe they are not trusted will never realize their full potential.

Leadership and Management in Balance

In our new post-heroic, globalized leadership environment, characterized by empowerment, excellence, and transformationalism, the difference between leadership and management takes on a new and important meaning. It has been said that people do not really want to be managed—they want to be led! Whoever heard of a world manager? World leader, yes; educational leader, political leader, scout leader, religious leader, business leader, quality leader–they all lead; they do not manage. You can lead a horse to water, but you cannot manage it to drink.

Though leadership and management are both crucial to achieving quality, they differ significantly. A key element in ensuring leadership for a durable organization is the institutional or corporate recognition that effective leadership is an art, not a hard science. Therefore, to accomplish it, one has to develop an intuitive understanding of what leadership really is and then learn to recognize when one is leading and when one is not. Unfortunately, some organizations are being micro-managed into the ground by well-meaning authorities who feel they are doing their jobs correctly by crawling into the weeds every day in every way. Since there is a critical difference between leadership and management in achieving success, a comparison of leaders and managers is appropriate. Leadership and management are neither synonymous nor interchangeable; they are both essential and cannot substitute for one another. But, what are the significant differences between the two?

Field Marshal Sir William Slim, who led the British Army in the reconquest of Burma from the Japanese in one of the epic campaigns of World War II, recognized the distinction when he said, " . . . managers are necessary; leaders are essential." "Leadership," Slim added, "is of the spirit, compounded of personality and vision, . . . management is of the mind, more a matter of accurate calculation, statistics, methods, time tables, and routine. . . ." In effect, this distinguished soldier maintained that leadership (spirit, personality, vision) is an effective *concept*, while management (mind, calculation, routine) is a cognitive *idea*. Modern organizations should give more attention to this important distinction. Survival leaders recognize the need for skilled managers, but they emphasize the need to focus more sharply on effective leadership qualities, lest too much energy be poured into doing the wrong things more efficiently.

In essence, management is the activity that allocates and utilizes resources to achieve organizational goals. Management is the physics of things; leadership is the chemistry of people. Leadership is the art of influencing people to accomplish an organization's purpose. Leaders are more concerned with effectiveness, foresight, and innovation while *doing the right things*. Managers are more interested in efficiency, current issues, and *doing things right*. While managers work *in* the system, leaders work *on* the system. Leaders use *emotional* and *spiritual* resources: values, commitment, and aspirations. Managers tend to employ *physical* resources of the organization: money, human skills, technology, and raw materials.

These two concepts, which are not independent but interdependent, can be further differentiated to achieve higher levels of success. Management involves planning, organizing, staffing, controlling, and problem solving. These processes both cause and produce organizational stability. For this reason, management can be characterized as a set of specific activities such as hiring a new employee to fill an existing position, defining required skills for various positions, and ensuring the availability of physical resources required to ensure efficient operation of any quality activity. Conversely, leadership sets direction, creates visions and values, and motivates and inspires people to change an organization's culture. Leaders light the way to the future and encourage people to achieve excellence; they model value-based principles. While leaders formulate, managers implement. Leaders have the capacity to lift the spirit of people and get organizations moving in new, more effective directions. Conceptually, leadership involves ideas about *what to do* rather than *how to do* things. It bridges the gap between the present and the future with imagination.

Focusing on Vision

Leaders who are able to survive globalization, six sigma competition, productive services, and e-business, provide the staying power to see a vision to its completion. They focus on vision with a laser-like intensity and allow no one to place limitations on them. These leaders use vision as a reference point to measure progress. They clearly sight their targets, especially in goal-related matters. Within this paradigm, leadership becomes a highly personal activity dealing principally with communications and interpersonal dynamics. The creative leader is a risk-taker and generalist, always searching for what is right while encouraging and welcoming change. Conversely, management is more impersonal. It deals largely with things and quantitative measures, the marshaling of required physical resources, and the control of activities needed to attain an organization's purpose. Managers work in the system; leaders work on the system.

Although management and leadership differ fundamentally, both are requisite in the pursuit of human accomplishment through continuous improvement. This analysis highlighting the differences between leadership and management in no way suggests that survival organizations do not need managers. Clearly, organizations need both leaders and managers since they simply perform different functions in achieving endurance. In today's highly competitive and changing world, organizations will require responsible leaders and managers at all levels who are willing and able to perform both of these behaviors equally well to achieve the desired high levels of results orientated activity.

Leadership and management go hand in hand; they are both needed to achieve organizational effectiveness in the war for survival. When practiced together, they provide the foundation from which a group draws inspiration, capability, and ultimately both efficiency and effectiveness. In reality, the organizational professional must be both a leader and a manager. But, the process begins with the leader articulating a clear mission, vision, and values. It is leadership, not management, that will move people in the direction of doing the right things. Leaders have the ability to encourage and inspire others to willingly follow into uncertain areas. They have a keen sense of what the problems are and can deal proactively with an ever-evolving reality.

Leaders frequently take a break from the rat race, stop for breath, and ask two key questions: What is our purpose? And what is our strategy toward its accomplishment? Survival leaders are unaffected by flattery, unswerved by opinion, and undismayed by apparent dilemmas. They face their work with a special brand of courage and hope–always keeping hope alive. Their life is ultimately crowned by achievement of worthy goals and exemplary service to others. This book, this *Survival Kit for Leaders*, with the key concepts discussed at length in Chapters 3 and beyond, is designed to be a lifeline to help you do just that. The future will be very competitive; learning how to lead is key to that future state. Understanding and applying leadership does not come easily, nor is the process always predictable. Leadership can be learned, but it requires considerable effort. As Gloria Steinem says, "There are learning moments. Things happen over and over again, and we learn in a spiral, not a straight line. And then one day we get it."

Discussion Questions and Ideas

- Has your workplace become a battleground? How is this war being waged? How extensively is the battle raging in your line of work?

- How can creative leaders (and employees) survive and even flourish in today's complex and challenging environment?

- Have you known particularly good or bad leaders and managers? Why do you judge them to be good or bad? What qualities and behaviors made them that way?

- How can we nurture creative pragmatists who can and will make our organizations more humane, productive, and long lasting?

- How can the leader contribute to a long-term commitment of the survival of an organization?

- In today's world of downsizing, restructuring, bankruptcy, cost-cutting, contracting-out, and a general absence of organizational loyalty, what hope is there that a leader can make a real difference?

Bibliography and Recommended Reading

Bennis, Warren. "The 4 Competencies of Leadership." *Training and Development Journal.* August 1984.

Brelin, Harvey K. "The Role of Leadership In Total Quality Improvement." *Continuous Journey.* December 1993-January 1994.

Capowski, Genevieve. "Anatomy of a Leader." *Management Review.* March 1994.

Gore, Al., Vice President. *Creating a Government That Works Better and Costs Less: Report of the National Performance Review.* Washington, D.C.: U.S. GPO, September 1993.

Hickman, Craig R. *A Manager's Mind. Soul of A Leader.* New York: Wiley, 1990.

Hogan, Robert, et al. "What We Know About Leadership." *American Psychologist.* June 1994.

Huey, John. "The New Post-Heroic Leadership." *Fortune.* February 1994.

Kotter, John P. *A Force for Change.* New York: Free Press, 1990.

Shaud, General John A., United States Air Force Retired. Interview by author. 29 April 1994 and 7 October 1994.

Slim, Field Marshal Sir William. *Defeat Into Victory.* London: Cassell and Company, Ltd, 1955.

Timpe, Dale A. *Leadership*. New York: Facts on File Publication, 1987.

Willis, Garry, "What Makes a Good Leader," *The Atlantic Monthly*, April 1994.

Zalenznik, Abraham. *Learning Leadership*. Chicago: Bowls Books, Inc., 1993.

Zenger, J. H., et al. *Leading Teams*. New York: Irwin, 1994.

Chapter 2

Survival Thoughts for Leaders

Executive Summary

The leader–at any level–is an easy target in today's jungle of downsizing, reorganizing, and reinventing. Digitization, globalization, and a host of other factors are transforming everything we do in organizations. How can the leader survive all these changes and still be a significant organizational asset? Survival for leaders today requires that leaders cope with the frenetic pace of change, and use that change as an ally. They must be able to inspire, excite and galvanize organizations through effective teamwork. These leaders set extraordinary goals–aim for the apparently "impossible" and exceed the expected. They act according to ethical standards, integrity, honesty, and with respect for the individual and group. They relish change and exemplify wisdom and good judgment. Leaders who survive invest in the development, retention, promotion, and motivation of their employees. They provide a workplace where commitment, creativity, respect, and diversity are valued and practiced. They also make extensive efforts to communicate with and encourage feedback from their followers.

Discussion

Just what is leadership? No clear-cut universally accepted definition of leadership has emerged. This book views leadership as an interpersonal process through which one individual influences the attitudes, beliefs, and especially the behavior of one or more other people. Emerging leadership is often characterized as inspirational. It is seen as bottom-up, transformational, visionary, values-oriented, developing and empowering. As Peter Drucker has correctly concluded: "An effective leader is not someone who is necessarily loved or admired. He or she is someone whose followers do the right things. Popularity is not leadership—results are." In today's world, leaders are highly visible and thus they must set the example for others to follow. These leaders are keenly aware that being responsible is a key factor in leading today. It is a deep sense of responsibility that distinguishes the leader from others with only intellect and skills. We agree with General Hal Hornburg, United States Air Force: "The first duty of a leader is to grow more leaders and that good leaders are teachers. They show us the way ahead and show how to get there. The general asserts that there are three basic types of leaders: Those who make organization better, those who make organization worse, and there are the caretakers." This book is intended to help leaders make it better.

Ever wonder what your people think about your leadership? Would they say it's too demanding, too out of touch? Would they want to do more for you if you gave them the opportunity? Do they share your values?

Leadership, like virtue, means different things to different people. Every serious student of the subject has a personal opinion about leadership. We readily admit to having no hidden or Olympian truths about leadership, only the desire to express some second thoughts that may be of some practical value for those who study, teach, and practice survival leadership.

Management and leadership are often considered the same activities, but the two concepts differ in the sense that leaders focus on people while managers deal with things. Field Marshal Sir William Slim, who from 1943 to 1945 led the 14th British Army in the reconquest of Burma from the Japanese in one of the epic campaigns of World War II, recognized this distinction when he said, "...managers are necessary; leaders are essential." Slim added that "...leadership is of the spirit, compounded of personality, and vision ...management is of the mind, more a matter of accurate calculation, statistics, methods, time tables, and routine...." In effect, this distinguished soldier maintained that leadership (spirit, personality, and vision) is an affective concept; management (mind, calculation, and routine) is a cognitive notion. Current organizations have not given enough attention to this important distinction. Although there are currently strong efforts to redress this imbalance between leadership and management, we have generally drifted too far toward management. This trend has been especially true in many training programs and practices.

Proliferation of management techniques in the business world and increasing demands for management expertise in other professions have confused many people with respect to the relationship between leadership and management. This chapter, and the remainder of this book, in the substantive chapters that follow, recognizes the need for skilled managers in organizations, but we need to focus more sharply on effective leadership qualities.

A familiar sign of the times in organizations today is the outcry for compelling and creative leadership. Some observers believe that the average American would be unable to respond should Martian spacemen land on American soil and demand, "Take us to your leader!" Most responsible people understand the management concept, but they have problems in the study of leadership because conceptually it is more difficult to comprehend. In fact, leadership in both a practical and theoretical sense is one of the most discussed and least understood subjects today. People in organizations tend to view leadership in much the same perspective as their health: They understand it best when they do not have it and feel a need for it.

Most people at one time or another have observed both successful and unsuccessful leaders. But the difference between successful and unsuccessful leaders is a matter of major importance for anyone who manages, develops, or conducts programs in leadership education. Professional development programs generally recognize leadership as the art of influencing and directing people in a manner that wins their obedience, confidence, respect, and enthusiastic cooperation in achieving a common objective. Professional educators and practitioners usually define a leader as a person who applies principles and techniques ensuring motivation, discipline, productivity, esprit, and effectiveness in dealing with people, tasks, and situations in order to accomplish the mission. Leadership is a quality–it provides vision; it deals with concepts; it seeks effectiveness; it exercises faith; it is an influence for good; it provides direction and thrives on finding opportunity.

Exercising Interpersonal Influence

People exercise leadership any time they attempt to change or modify the behavior of an individual or a group of individuals. They do not walk by a problem, are experts on "hot-button" issues, and insist on standards and are solution-oriented. Leaders seek to exercise interpersonal influence through their persuasive power and acceptance by followers in given situations. To understand the nature of leadership, one must first understand the nature of power, for leadership is a special form of power involving relationships with people. To develop these relationships, leaders must successfully fuse organizational and personal needs in a way that permits people and organizations to reach peaks of mutual achievement and satisfaction. James MacGregor Burns states that "Leadership is nothing if not linked to a collective purpose." Thus, leaders get things done through people and make things work. Trained in this context, leaders are facilitators who help to pave the way toward the achievement of goals.

Although effective leaders are goal-oriented, they have other basic responsibilities. They must have the necessary influence and communication skills to express and interpret the mission so clearly their followers can easily understand and accept it. The key word is focus. The leader's primary task is to focus the attention of people he or she hopes to influence. This critical leadership skill requires clear understanding of the goal or mission to ensure a logical sequence of actions for getting the job done. They strive to keep tasks in line with resources and know what things cost. Survival leaders are personally engaged and find all available options.

Some people believe that leadership can be taught, but others contend that an individual can only be taught about leadership. If education is perceived as a change in behavior through experience, and effective leadership as a set of behaviors applicable to given situations, then survival leadership can indeed be taught. Despite the complexity of the leadership role, it can be learned when there is a definite willingness to expend the required time and resources. Much the same as lawyers, writers, test pilots, or engineers, leaders are generally not born, but developed. Leadership is a vital part of today's professional development. That is why leadership education is emphasized in so many institutions. People can develop and learn leadership just as they learn any other complex skill, but the learning process requires intensive effort, study, and continuing application. Organizations should continuously seek out latent talent and then train to full potential to develop effective leaders. The subsequent chapters in this book would be a good place to begin.

Differentiate Leadership Elements

One requirement of that development process is to differentiate three major leadership elements. These are the leader, the follower, and the situation. Leadership studies should emphasize that in acceptance of their professional obligations and positions of authority, personnel should demonstrate leadership qualities in all their activities. They should understand that leadership within an organization can be a most rewarding and exciting experience. Although the primary challenge is successful mission accomplishment, instructors should emphasize that successful leaders must never overlook the welfare of their people, for people are indeed an organization's most important asset. Lectures and case studies should accent the fact that leaders must be prepared to make many difficult and complex decisions, sometimes on a daily basis.

Instruction of this sort should also focus on the fact that leaders are judged for the most part on the timeliness and soundness of their decisions. Knowledge gained through experience, job-related reading, professional development education, and specialized training is invaluable. But common sense gained through experience is the key to practical and productive leadership.

The following paragraphs contain some thoughts that may be helpful in developing and presenting leadership instruction.

People cannot lead effectively from the privacy of their offices. True leaders visit their people on the job and observe their working conditions firsthand. Highly visible leaders leave their footprints everywhere in the organization. One cannot be a lone wolf and expect to lead the pack.

The days of blind obedience, unlimited resources, and blank checks have passed. The all-volunteer military force only underscores the need for leadership skills that ensure creativity, efficiency, productivity, and vitality in an environment constantly faced with complex challenges. To meet these challenges, survival leaders must know their people, their problems, interests, and needs. Also, today's leader must understand that young people now are more sophisticated, better educated, more politically aware and more conscious of disciplinary limits. As a rule, these young men and women are not motivated by intimidation; they must be led, rather than driven. The responsibility of the leader is to instill in these people a sense of purpose, obligation, work ethic, and loyalty. Leaders need to counteract careerism, which in essence means the desire to be, rather than the desire to do. The slacker's wish to be in the right (i.e., cushy) job at the right time needs to be replaced with devotion to responsibility and commitment. Leaders at every level must understand that leadership is a subjective chemistry filled with human variables. Too few have the ability to motivate others through commanding presence, personal force, and example.

Survival leaders are demanding of themselves and their subordinates. Their style is a blend of caring, dignity, discipline, and self-confidence rooted in unshakable dedication to their people, their organization, and the mission they serve. The word "caring" has special meaning for effective leaders, since with caring they must comprehend and negotiate a special mixture of frustration and difficulty. Ample evidence proves that something so simple as caring improves leadership and that it can be contagious.

Quantitative and Qualitative Accomplishment

Effective leaders concentrate on quantitative and qualitative accomplishment. All too often, people in leadership positions concern themselves with quantity of work their subordinates perform and not with the quality of that product. Leaders recognize no substitutes for productive work, intense concentration, and willingness to assume total responsibility. Acceptance of leadership responsibilities requires time, total effort, and intelligence–a state of complete dedication. But, even though leadership requires total effort, leaders alone cannot achieve their goals. They must develop and recognize their subordinates if excellence is expected over an extended period.

Leaders must delegate tasks, which require their people to make decisions. The true test of senior leadership is the behavior reflected among their subordinates. Thus, followers need to be involved as the first step toward commitment. Good leaders realize that in a digitized world, bureaucracy must be reformed. Bloated bureaucracies frustrate people, distort their priorities, limit their dreams, and turn the focus of an entire enterprise inward. Better leaders see bureaucracies for what they are: slow, self-absorbed, customer insensitive and counterproductive in a fast paced world. Bureaucracies of this kind simply help us trudge up our own private Calvary.

Leadership education should reflect a deeper historical perspective in a relative sense to the lives and accomplishments of such leaders as Washington, Lincoln, Churchill, Roosevelt, Gandhi and Einstein. We should make a better attempt to link theory with practice by reflecting on the lives and accomplishments of these and other leaders. Let us also not forget leaders such as Bob Galvin, Nelson Mandela, Martin Luther King, Jr., Jack Welch, Helen Keller, and Gloria Steinem. These are only a few of the many outstanding leaders worthy of intensive study. We need to especially understand why these leaders mattered and why they made and make such a difference. Their contributions to society should clearly be included in our leadership curricula. The best leadership lab is life itself. Watching leaders you admire is a great lesson and a productive way to learn.

Winston Churchill, Britain's wartime prime minister and one of the all-time great leaders, employed principles of strong and decisive leadership in guiding his people through the dark days of World War II. Although he was an able manager, his greatness stemmed from his ability to motivate, inspire, and give of himself–this is true leadership. He had more to offer than mere planning, programming, and management by objectives; he offered blood, toil, tears, and sweat. Perhaps his greatest contribution was his clear, eloquent, and moving public articulation of the situation and its requirements. He focused on the problem and then did something about it. During World War II, Churchill mobilized words and sent them into battle.

Leadership instruction should stress that development of effective leaders is easier said than done because leadership requires tremendous inner strength, character, and purpose. Unfortunately, we do not live in a time of the simple solution. Successful leaders do not speak in terms of simple explanations, but rather of hard choices. There are no simple solutions or "trick shots" in developing sound leadership qualities. This book is no exception, no quick-fix panacea for all of life's most intractable problems. Sorry. We must work continually at it and constantly strive to achieve it. Thus, educational programs should be more reality-centered and should address down-to-earth, nitty-gritty aspects of leadership not only in lectures but also in instructor-controlled discussions, practical exercises, role-playing, research projects, case studies, and, most importantly, in leadership laboratories. The discussion questions at the end of each substantive chapter in this book are part of that practical paradigm. Please use them!

Leadership instruction should focus on the key element–people. If leaders ignore individual needs and dignity, they not only cheapen their leadership quality but risk duplicating the ideological mistakes of those leaders for whom the individual is merely a tool or pawn. Closely related to this idea is the implication that leaders should place a high priority on meaningful, mutually rewarding integration of the total work force.

Instruction should also include a clear, simple, customer-centered vision. The intent is to create an environment of growth, excitement, informality, and celebration of results. This should result in effective mechanisms for dealing with the speed of change and creating an atmosphere that energizes others.

Leadership styles resemble fingerprints in the sense that each is different and highly individualistic. Thus, in studying leadership styles, people should learn how to sort the good from the bad, the effective from the ineffective, from the perspective of their *own* unique personal qualities and circumstances. Through this process of sifting and selecting, through the lens of their own eyes, they can begin to develop the basics of their own leadership styles. Whatever the style, it should be predicated on motivation, sensitivity, and appropriate consideration for both human relationships (concern for people) and tasks (concern for productivity) within the framework of a given organizational environment.

Behavioral Science Approach

Leaders should apply the behavioral science approach to enhance effective behavior. They should also stress the pluralistic view of motivation to show that follower behavior stems from many different types of need. The approach to task consideration should address who, what, when, where, why, and how specific tasks will be accomplished. They should establish well-defined, realistic patterns of organization, channels of communication, ways of getting jobs done, making difficult decisions, the ability to consistently execute, building self-confidence and simplicity. Simplicity leads to speed, one of the key drivers of cooperate success.

Leaders should also play key roles in identifying extra dimensions of leadership uniquely applicable to organizational members. Much of the problem in leadership today is that the majority of conceptual models, cases, and studies are based on outdated or overly theoretical, ivory-towerish research and experience. Aspiring leaders should identify and internalize leadership variables uniquely characteristic of their own organizational and personal setting.

A key component of leadership is the decision-making process, including problem analysis. Although in some sense everyone already knows how to think, we can all learn how to think more creatively, more logically, and more effectively. We can learn to sift, sort, and process increasingly larger quantities of information that too often threaten to smother us in an avalanche of data. Leaders should also address and analyze the following individual leadership characteristics:

1. **Sense of Responsibility:** People who aspire to high positions must subordinate their personal desires (and at times even the desires of their families) to that of the organization. The late Mamie Eisenhower once stated she knew she had to take second place to the army. The leader recognizes responsibility and relishes it as a vehicle to display leadership skills.

2. **Technical and Professional Competence:** Subordinates will give a leader a reasonable period to get his or her "feet on the ground," but they will not respect the individual who continually relies on others to make decisions or provide guidance. Leaders must give evidence to their people of the leadership knowledge and capability they possess. A leader's title, rank, and/or position will not ensure that subordinates will follow or trust the leader in

any situation. At the moment of truth, they follow the leader who knows! Therefore, leaders must learn all details of the technical and tactical aspects of their job.

3. **Emotional Stability:** Leaders must exercise self-control if they expect to control others and must maintain control in the most trying situations. Furthermore, they should strive to govern their personal lives and should never allow personal problems to color decisions or spawn adverse situational reactions.

4. **Enthusiasm:** A leader must be genuinely enthusiastic in all the tasks comprising the organization mission. Followers will automatically give more of themselves and take more pride in their work when they know their leader is actively involved, personally invested, and dedicated. Some leaders are reluctant to delve into functional areas where they have no prior experience or qualifications. Often effective leaders never feel fully qualified for the job they hold. It is important that a leader seek new directions and explore unfamiliar areas.

5. **Listening:** A good leader is not an interruptaholic, but listens. Listening involves much more than mere hearing. Successful leaders squint with their ears. They interpret and carefully evaluate what they hear and do not permit personal ideas, emotions, or prejudices to distort what a person says. Disciplined listening prevents them from tuning out subjects they personally consider too complex or uninteresting. Effective listening is difficult, but it is a key communication skill too rarely emphasized in leadership education. Effective listening adds a special dimension to what leaders can achieve. It is surprising what two well-disciplined ears can do.

6. **Self-image:** All leaders must have positive self-images formed through objective perception and interpretation of their environment. Self-images are controlling factors in behavior because all people act as they perceive themselves. Leaders must develop self-esteem and personal values and in relating to authority should feel they be-

long in the role of boss. Leaders must be honest and fair with themselves about personal strengths and weaknesses.

7. **Ethics and Integrity:** Ethics plays a key role in the leadership function because it is the basis of all group interaction and decision-making. Professional ethics requires leaders to maintain high personal conduct standards and to adhere to those standards in all situations so followers can rely on leader actions. Personal integrity is an important element of one's ethics. Regardless of rank or position, leaders demonstrate integrity when their concern for organizational interests is always greater than their personal pride and when they hold themselves to the same standards even when their superiors are not present. Integrity establishes the trust that is so critical in the human relationships that make our values work. With trust, employees can take risks and believe us when we say a "miss" does not mean career damage. One "aw shucks" should not outweigh a career full of "good on yous," but your people will never believe this unless you prove it to them! Survival leaders tie ethics and values together conceptually. They understand that ethics are standards by which leaders should act based on values and that values are core beliefs. They believe that integrity is first, believe in service before self, and they provide excellence in all they do. Values motivate attitudes and actions, and, with ethics, show us right from wrong.

8. **Recognition:** Leaders recognize the accomplishments of their people. The philosopher William James provided sage advice when he said, "The deepest principle in human nature is to be appreciated." The inability to satisfy needs for informal recognition seems to be a common shortcoming of many authority figures that seem more problem-and task-oriented than people-oriented. The more we share the credit, the more there will be to share credit for.

9. **Flexibility:** A leader must understand that no two people or situations are ever exactly alike. Yesterday's approach may or may not be the correct approach for today or to-

morrow. Effective leaders adapt their approaches to the particular person/group or problems at hand. In dealing with problems and situations, leaders should always be ready to refine or modify their approach and response. There will always be new challenges, as well as new tools, resources, and methods available to those creative, insightful, and brave enough to use them. Leaders must devote much thought and effort to understanding the nature of change; they should have the ability to take, proactively, whatever comes their way and thrive on it.

10. **Humor:** Leaders should have a sense of humor because they set the tone for their organizations. When a leader smiles, it is easier for others to smile, relax, and focus. A smile is a curve that can set many things straight! Most people prefer to belong to a relaxed and pleasant organization rather than to one laden with tension. Genuine, appropriate, good-natured humor can be a positive and welcome attribute in all organizations and can make many things more tolerable.

11. **Risk:** Leaders prefer working from high-risk positions; indeed, they often are temperamentally disposed to seek out risk and danger, especially where opportunity and reward appear high. A leader must be a risk-taker. If leaders could perform without risk, their jobs would be much easier, but risk-taking is inherent in survival leadership. Without risk there is no action, no achievement. President Theodore Roosevelt eloquently addressed this subject: "Far better it is to dare mighty things, to win glorious triumphs, even though checkered by failure, than to take rank with those poor spirits who neither enjoy much nor suffer much because they live in the great twilight that knows neither victory nor defeat." Virtually all leaders worthy of the name lean heavily on that inspiration in times of high risk. Leadership is a risk endeavor, a win-or-lose game, and many of its ingredients must be so.

12. **Communication Skill:** Effective communications is a key leadership variable. Verbal/nonverbal and written communications are essential in acquiring follower coopera-

tion. Communication is the adhesive that holds an organization together, so to say no person can lead if he or she cannot communicate is to belabor the obvious. As Benjamin Disraeli put it, "Men govern with words." This means keeping your people informed. A well-informed subordinate will have a better attitude toward his or her leader.

13. **Vision:** Leaders need a visual image of where they see the organization going and how it can get there. Vision is essential to organizational progress. As the *Koran* says, "If you do not know where you are going, any road will get you there." Without this commitment, leaders can be held hostage to the emotions of the moment. Furthermore, effective leaders project ideas and images that excite people and develop choices that are timely and appropriate for the situation at hand. Therefore, a dominant characteristic of effective leaders is their ability to create enthusiasm for work that will reach far beyond the myriad distractions and annoyances of day-to-day life and stay focused on the overarching vision.

14. **Courage:** Leaders view courage as an essential binding influence for unity of action. Followers will usually excuse almost any stupidity, indiscretion, or ill-conceived action, but they will not accept excessive timidity. This was the essence of Captain Queeg's failure in *The Caine Mutiny*. Whimsical, eccentric, and an oppressor of men, Queeg would have become tolerable had he (under fire) acquitted himself with courage. Conversely, Alexander the Great overcame deep personal flaws such as paranoia and megalomania and won both phenomenal loyalty from his troops and unparalleled conquests, largely because of his incredible courage in battle. In holding strong to fundamental leadership principles, effective leaders see themselves under a continuous challenge to prove by one means or another the quality and character of their person. Courage is indispensable if leaders expect to give direction to the lives of other people.

15. **Energy:** Both mental and physical energy are necessary elements of successful leadership. Good leaders always seem ready for action, and they know how to pace themselves. Many survival leaders have learned that if they exercise regularly and watch their diet, they can generate more energy than they may think possible. These leaders seemingly inexhaustible source of renewable energy stems, as well, from the other aspects of leadership as leaders draw power from their commitment, vision, strength, and courage. For the true leader, his or her life's mission is not truly work. It is rather a passion, a literal labor of love. Like a star, it supplies its own energy.

16. **Perseverance:** People who aspire to or have achieved leadership are those who persevere in their work. Persistence in an undertaking in spite of counterinfluences, opposition, or discouragement is central to the personality of an effective leader. Survival leaders aren't born—they persevere. The value of perseverance is critical to a leader's success.

17. **Altruism:** Leaders should not use their position for personal and special privileges. Their only privilege should be to serve and to discharge their responsibilities in accordance with the highest traditions of the leader. Any person (regardless of official position, title, or position) can lead if he or she has the courage, the ability, and the desire to serve others. In effect, leadership is a call to service. A leader fixated on personal self-aggrandizement is no leader at all but is a parasite.

18. **Decision-making:** Leaders must be able to make correct estimates of a given situation and then use this basis to make sound decisions. Leaders are decisive, and their decisions are made with logic, rationality, and proper consideration for all relevant factors. Although sometimes an educated guess is the best option, leaders ensure that these guesses are very well educated indeed, with the equivalent of a Harvard diploma, before they send them out into the world.

19. **Knowledge of Your People:** Leaders need to know and understand their subordinates. If followers know their leaders are concerned about them, they are more likely to become the type of people on which the leader can depend. And knowledge of the individual strengths and shortcomings, aspirations and fears, preferences and aversions of each person is an essential element in the leader's tool kit.

20. **Set the Example.** Organizational standards are set by leader example. "Follow me and do as I do" is an excellent guide to the way leaders should act. If people never see the leader out from behind the desk, and never witness the leader actually *doing* anything, how can they be inspired?

The message is clear. Leaders are not given esteem with their rank or assignments; they earn it by manifesting leadership characteristics. They first create a tolerant environment, develop respect, and finally win the esteem of their superiors, peers, and subordinates. It is not an easy task, but the personal satisfaction and sense of contribution and achievement are great and well worth the effort.

Of all the distinct qualities characteristic of effective leaders, the most important quality is moral leadership. Omar Bradley, General of the Army during World War II, probably said it best, "We have grasped the mystery of the atom and rejected the Sermon on the Mount. The world has achieved brilliance without wisdom, power without conscience. Ours is a world of nuclear giants and ethical infants." There is a profound need for leaders to address the moral, uplifting, and transcending aspects of leadership. This implies a leadership of purpose, broad direction, and strong commitment, for through these, people can better appreciate and understand the values holding organizations together today.

Leaders have the fearsome ability to lead followers down the path to personal and organizational decay, if that is their inclination. But positive leadership can take people to higher values and purposes. Thus, leadership is neither inherently good nor bad, but it can be a strong influence in either direction. As you read the substantive chapters of this book, beginning with the next one, please actively search for answers to such questions as who are the leaders and who are the followers? Who is leading whom to where? For what purpose? With what results? For better, or for worse?

In summary, the thoughts expressed in this chapter have many ancillary facets, which could be further developed. This chapter in *Survival Kit for Leaders* has pointed out the more central and basic elements for leadership survival. We would suspect that most of you reading this book would acknowledge and perhaps even agree with, the thoughts presented here. But unless you take concrete action to put these thoughts into practice, they will be of little practical value. Knowledge does not become power until used. In our harsh world torn between conflicting ideologies and increasingly cut-throat, competitive enterprise, leadership will continue to play an ever more vital role. Each of us should be prepared to make our own contribution. If we work hard, stick to the basics, and strive for effective execution, great strides can be made in improving our leadership. It would be helpful for aspiring leaders to understand that strength of character can carry them a long way in influencing other people and that, for a leader, strength of character is a force multiplier. The best leaders work hard to ensure that they and their followers stay in shape mentally, physically, and spiritually. This is almost essential if they are to mentor, coach, and lead.

Discussion Questions and Ideas

- In your own words define leadership. What is your leadership philosophy?

- Are leadership and management fundamentally the same? If there are differences: What are the distinctions? Can one person be both at the same time? Do some organizations need more of one than the other?

- Are leaders born or developed? Is leadership an art or science? Do you believe leadership can be taught, and if so, how?

- Can there be such a thing as an effective leader who is also a bad person? In this regard, how would you categorize Alexander the Great, Napoleon Bonaparte, and Adolf Hitler?

- Do leaders need other leaders?

- Is it true that a leader is someone who makes things happen, or does a leader react effectively to things that happen independent of the leader?

- In your judgment, what are the key leadership characteristics? Do you disagree with any of the characteristics identified in this chapter? Would you substitute others?

- How do leaders set the tone for everything we do?

Bibliography and Recommended Reading

Avolio, Burce J. *Full Leadership* London: Sage, 1999.

Lester, R., Morton, G. *Concepts for Air for Leadership.*
Air University Press (Maxwell AFB, Al), 2001.

Chapter 3

Profile of a Leader

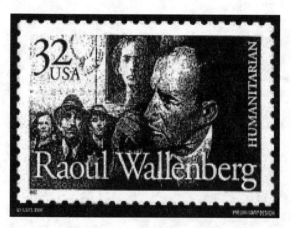

The United States Postal Service released a stamp to honor the memory of Raoul Wallenberg.

Executive Summary

This is a study of the leadership principles employed by Raoul Wallenberg, a Swedish civilian citizen of considerable personal wealth who went to Budapest in 1944 to intervene on behalf of Hungary's 700,000 Jews who were being deported by the Nazis to extermination camps. This extended case narrative profiles the extraordinary accomplishments of a truly unique leader.

Wallenberg is credited with having saved close to 100,000 lives. On 5 October 1981, the President and Congress recognized Wallenberg's contribution to humanity when they named him only the second person ever to be awarded honorary United States citizenship; the other is Winston Churchill. By joint resolution, the United States Congress also designated 5 October 1989 as Raoul Wallenberg Day. In addition, the street in front of the Holocaust Memorial Museum in Washington, D.C., has been renamed Raoul Wallenberg Plaza.

Leaders create a new reality for the purpose they serve. This case study is intended to demonstrate how Wallenberg exercised leadership and how he refused to be indifferent, complacent, or ignorant of the suffering of others. Wallenberg emerges from a sordid chapter in human history as a courageous and compassionate leader–a symbol of the best mankind has to offer.

Discussion

During the waning months of World War II, the Allies were desperate for ways to stop Hitler's slaughter of innocent civilians in Eastern Europe. Even as the prospects for an Axis military victory dimmed, the Nazis grew more determined to complete the "final solution." Death camps operated at maximum capacity in a feverish effort to rid Europe of Jews and other target groups. Until a complete military triumph could be secured, the Allies were powerless to halt the genocide raging on behind enemy lines. Therefore, a volunteer was sought–someone who could go where Allied tanks and aircraft could not and disrupt the insidious Nazi death machine.

No one could have been a less obvious choice for this mission than Raoul Wallenberg. Wallenberg was thirty-two years old in 1944, a wealthy upper class Swede from a prominent, well-respected family. Sweden's neutrality in the war was only one in a long series of ready-made excuses life had handed young Wallenberg, had he wanted to use them to refuse the rescue mission. He was not Jewish; he was rich; he was well connected politically; he was in line to take the helm of the vast Wallenberg financial empire; he had everything to lose and nothing to gain by accepting this challenge.

Wallenberg was recommended for this endeavor by Koloman Lauer, a business partner who was involved with the new War Refugee Board. Lauer felt that Raoul possessed the proper combination of dedication, skill, and courage, despite his youth and inexperience, and that his family name would afford him some protection. Wallenberg proved eager to serve, but he boldly demanded and was granted a great deal of latitude in the methods he would use.

When he learned that Adolf Eichmann was transporting roughly 10,000-12,000 Hungarian Jews to the gas chambers each day, Wallenberg hastily prepared to travel to Budapest. His "cover" was that of a diplomat, with the official title of first secretary of the Swedish legation. He conceived a plan whereby false Swedish passports (Schutzpasse) would be created and used to give potential victims safe passage out of Nazi-controlled territory. In conjunction with this, a series of safe houses would be established within Hungary in the guise of official Swedish legation buildings under diplomatic protection. With this scheme still forming in his mind, "Swedish diplomat" Wallenberg entered Hungary at the request of the United States War Refugee Board and his own government on 6 July 1944 with a mission of saving as many Hungary's Jews as possible from Nazi liquidation.

He designed the fake passports himself. They were masterpieces of the type of formal, official-appearing pomp that was so impressive to the Nazis. Wallenberg, though young, had traveled and studied extensively abroad, both in the United States (where he attended the University of Michigan as a student of architecture) and in Europe, and he knew how to deal with people and get things done. He worked hard at understanding enemies as well as allies, to know what motivated them, what they admired, what they feared, what they respected. He correctly concluded that the Nazis and Hungarian fascists (Arrow Cross) with whom he would be dealing responded best to absolute authority and official status. He used this principle in fashioning his passports as well as in his personal encounters with the enemy.

Cultivating Others to Help

Wallenberg began with forty important contacts in Budapest and quickly cultivated others who were willing to help. It is estimated that under Wallenberg's leadership he and his associates distributed Swedish passports to 20,000 of Budapest's Jews and protected 13,000 more in safe houses that he rented and which flew the Swedish flag. However, Eichmann continued to pursue his own mission with fanatical zealous devotion, and the death camps roared around the clock. Trains packed with people, crammed eighty to a cattle car, with nothing but a little water and a bucket for waste, constantly made the four-day journey from Budapest to Auschwitz and back again. The Hungarian countryside was already devoid of Jews, and the situation in the last remaining urban enclaves was critical. And so Wallenberg himself plunged into the midst of the struggle.

Sandor Ardai was sent by the Jewish underground to drive for Wallenberg; Ardai later told of one occasion when Wallenberg intercepted a trainload of Jews about to leave for Auschwitz. Wallenberg swept past the SS officer who ordered him to depart. In Ardai's words,

> Then he climbed up on the roof of the train and began handing in protective passes through the doors that were not yet sealed. He ignored orders from the Germans for him to get down. Then the Arrow Cross men began shooting and shouting at him to go away. He ignored them and calmly continued handing out passports to the hands that were reaching out for them. I believe the Arrow Cross men deliberately aimed over his head, as not one shot hit him, which would have been impossible otherwise. I think this is what they did because they were so impressed by his courage. After Wallenberg had handed over the last of the passports, he ordered all those who had one to leave the train and walk to the caravan of cars parked nearby, all marked in Swedish colours. I don't remember exactly how many, but he saved dozens off that train, and the Germans and Arrow Cross were so dumbfounded they let him get away with it! (Bierman 91)

As the war situation deteriorated for the Germans, Eichmann diverted trains from the death camp routes for more direct use in supplying troops. But all this meant for his victims was that they now had to walk to their destruction. In November 1944, Eichmann ordered the 125-mile death marches, and the raw elements soon combined with deprivation of food and sleep to turn the roadside from Budapest to the camps into one massive graveyard. Wallenberg made frequent visits to the stopping areas to do what he could. In one instance, Wallenberg announced his arrival with all the authority he could muster, and then,

> *"You there!"* The Swede pointed to an astonished man, waiting for his turn to be handed over to the executioner. *"Give me your Swedish passport and get in that line,"* he barked. *"And you, get behind him. I know I issued you a passport."* Wallenberg continued, moving fast, talking loud, hoping the authority in his voice would somewhat rub off on these defeated people. . . . The Jews finally caught on. They started groping in pockets for bits of identification. A driver's license or birth certificate seemed to do the trick. The Swede was grabbing them so fast; the Nazis, who couldn't read Hungarian anyway, didn't seem to be checking. Faster, Wallenberg's eyes urged them, faster, before the game is up. In minutes he had several hundred people in his convoy. International Red Cross trucks, there at Wallenberg's behest, arrived and the Jews clambered on. . . . Wallenberg jumped into his own car. He leaned out of the car window and whispered, *"I am sorry,"* to the people he was leaving behind. *"I am trying to take the youngest ones first;"* he explained. *"I want to save a nation."* (Marton 110:11)

This type of action worked many times. Wallenberg and his aides would encounter a death march, and, while Raoul shouted orders for all those with Swedish protective passports to raise their hands, his assistants ran up and down the prisoners' ranks telling them to raise their hands whether or not they had a document. Wallenberg "then claimed custody of all who had raised their hands and such was his bearing that none of the Hungarian guards opposed him. The extraordinary thing was the absolutely convincing power of his behavior," according to Joni Moser (Quoted in Bierman 90).

Wallenberg indirectly helped many who never even saw his face because as his deeds were talked about, they inspired hope, courage, and action in many people who otherwise felt powerless to escape destruction. He became a symbol of good in a part of the world dominated by evil and a reminder of the hidden strengths within each human spirit.

Tommy Lapid was thirteen years old in 1944 when he was one of 900 people crowded fifteen or twenty to a room in one of the Swedish safe houses. His account illustrates not only vintage Wallenberg tactics but also how Wallenberg epitomized hope and righteousness and how his influence extended throughout the land as a beacon to those engulfed in the darkness of despair.

> One morning, a group of these Hungarian Fascists came into the house and said all the able-bodied women must go with them. We knew what this meant. My mother kissed me and I cried and she cried. We knew we were parting forever and she left me there, an orphan to all intents and purposes. Then, two or three hours later, to my amazement, my mother returned with the other women. It seemed like a mirage, a miracle. My mother was there–she was alive and she was hugging me and kissing me, and she said one word: *"Wallenberg."* I knew who she meant because Wallenberg was a legend among the Jews. In the complete and total hell in which we lived, there was a savior-angel somewhere, moving around. After she had composed herself, my

mother told me that they were being taken
to the river when a car arrived and out
stepped Wallenberg–and they knew immediately who it was because there was only
one such person in the world. He went up
to the Arrow Cross leader and protested that
the women were under his protection. They
argued with him, but he must have had incredible charisma, some great personal authority, because there was absolutely nothing behind him, nothing to back him up.
He stood out there in the street, probably
feeling the loneliest man in the world, trying to pretend there was something behind
him. They could have shot him then and
there in the street and nobody would have
known about it. Instead, they relented and
let the women go. (Bierman 88-89)

Virtually alone in the middle of enemy territory, out-
numbered and outgunned beyond belief, Wallenberg worked
miracles on a daily basis. His weapons were courage,
self-confidence, ingenuity, understanding of his adversaries,
and ability to inspire others to achieve the goals he set. His
leadership was always in evidence. The Nazis and Arrow Cross
did not know how to deal with such a man. Here was someone thickly cloaked in apparent authority, but utterly devoid
of actual political or military power. Here was a man who
was everything they wished they could be in terms of personal strength of character but for the fact that he was their polar
opposite in purpose.

It is impossible to calculate precisely how many people
Raoul Wallenberg directly or indirectly saved from certain
death. Some estimate the number as close to 100,000, and
countless more may have survived in part because of the hope

and determination they derived from his leadership and example (House of Representatives Report, Ninety-Sixth Congress, 2-3). Additionally, he inspired other neutral embassies and the International Red Cross office in Budapest to join in his efforts to protect the Jews. But the desperate days just prior to the Soviet occupation of Budapest presented Wallenberg with his greatest challenge and most astonishing triumph.

Eichmann planned to finish the extermination of the remaining 100,000 Budapest Jews in one enormous massacre; if there were no time to ship them to the death camps, then he would let their own neighborhoods become their slaughterhouses. To cheat the Allies out of at least part of their victory, he would order some 500 SS men and a large number of Arrow Cross to ring the ghetto and murder the Jews right there. Wallenberg learned of this plot through his network of contacts and tried to intimidate some lower-ranking authorities into backing down, but with the Soviets on their doorsteps, many ceased to care what happened to them. His only hope, and the only hope for the 100,000 surviving Jews, was the overall commander of the SS troops, General August Schmidthuber.

Wallenberg sent a message to Schmidthuber stating that if the massacre took place, he would ensure Schmidthuber was held personally responsible and would see him hanged as a war criminal. The bluff worked. The slaughter was called off, and the city fell out of Nazi hands soon thereafter when the Soviet troops rolled in. Thus, tens of thousands were saved in this one incident alone.

But, while peace came to Europe, Wallenberg's fate took a very different path. He vanished, and the whole truth of what happened to him has not been revealed even to this day. From various sources, though, the following seems to have occurred.

Wallenberg Taken into Custody

The Soviets took Wallenberg into custody when they occupied Budapest, probably because they suspected him of being an anti-Soviet spy. For a decade, they denied any involvement in Wallenberg's disappearance. Then they admitted having incarcerated him but claimed he died in prison of a heart attack in 1947. He would have been thirty-five years old. Since then, however, many people who have served time in Soviet prison have reported seeing Wallenberg, conversing with him, or communicating with him through tap codes. Others have heard of him and his presence in the prisons but had no direct contact. The Soviets have denied the accuracy of all of these reports and have never deviated from their official position. But in 1989, Soviet officials met with members of Wallenberg's family and turned over some of his personal effects. Reportedly, a genuine investigation was launched in an effort to determine the truth. Since then, conflicting bits of information have come from former members of the KGB and others, tending to confirm or contradict the official version of Wallenberg's fate. Whether the years and the prisons will ever yield up their secrets to reveal the whole truth remains to be seen.

Today in Israel there is a grove of trees, planted by the Martyrs' and Heroes' Remembrance Authority, or *Yad Vashem*. Known as *The Avenue of the Righteous,* each tree memorializes a "righteous Gentile," someone who risked his or her life to help Jews during the Holocaust. The trees stand in silent testament to those who, in the words of a former speaker of Israel's parliament, "saved not only the Jews but the honor of Man" (Bierman viii). Along with Raoul Wallenberg's tree, there is a medal. His medal bears the language of the Talmud and summarizes his mission in the words, "Whoever saves a single soul, it is as if he had saved the whole world."

The chairman of *Yad Vashem*, Gideon Hausner, who also prosecuted Adolf Eichmann, summarized his feelings for Raoul Wallenberg in this way:

> Here is a man who had the choice of remaining in secure, neutral Sweden when Nazism was ruling Europe. Instead, he left this haven and went to what was then one of the most perilous places in Europe, Hungary. And for what? To save Jews. He won his battle and I feel that in this age when there is so little to believe in—so very little on which our young people can pin their hopes and ideals—he is a person to show to the world, which knows so little about him. That is why I believe the story of Raoul Wallenberg should be told and his figure, in all its true proportions, projected into human minds. (Bierman viii-ix)

There is much we all can learn from Raoul Wallenberg's life. Young and old alike need heroes, role models, people to remind us of the immensity of human potential for good in the midst of evil. The United States Congress recognized this when it made Wallenberg only the second person ever to be awarded honorary United States citizenship; the other is Winston Churchill. On that occasion, one television news commentator spoke for millions when he said, "It is human beings such as Raoul Wallenberg who make life worth living."

Leaders at every level can make use of Wallenberg's life and example to enhance their ability to inspire, to motivate, and to succeed. Leadership is difficult to define, but "you know it when you see it." Looking at Wallenberg's heroic work in Hungary, one sees leadership in action. We will now more closely examine his leadership style. There are several elements of what we shall call "The Wallenberg Effect" which can be adapted and incorporated into each leader's own personal style and situation.

1. Knowledge

Wallenberg's success was largely based upon the knowledge of his enemies, of resources available to both sides, of the limits as to what was permissible, and of himself. This information enables a leader to understand each situation within a context that will allow a reasoned course of action. This is why knowing the facts and the substantive details surrounding issues has always been and always will be an integral part of a leader's decision-making and problem-solving ability.

The traditional types of information gathered, such as planned actions, location, movement, numerical strength, type and condition of circumstances, and availability of material resources are obviously important. But Wallenberg proved the utility of subtler information as well. Because he understood the way his enemies thought and felt, because he comprehended what motivated them, he knew which buttons to push in each individual situation. He knew the great deference to authority and the fear of those in positions of power that were part of the Nazi and Arrow Cross mentality. This enabled him to bluff them with his false passports and with his air of officialdom so as to achieve excellent, seemingly impossible results. Wallenberg had a commanding presence, which is a hallmark of the effective leader but that presence was fortified with the knowledge of how he would be perceived by his adversaries.

He also understood the rules of the game he was playing, as they applied to him, his associates, and their opponents. In effect, Wallenberg was very much a situational leader. He was able to adapt his behavior to meet the demands of the unique circumstances that confronted him. This is why he demanded and obtained authority from the Allies to use deception, bribery, and threats, and to invoke Swedish immunity as needed. He was in an environment where such tactics were the rule rather than the exception; they worked for others, and he knew he could make them work for him. As a leader, Wallenberg was out front, not hiding behind a desk or behind bureaucratic inertia. He showed initiative. He responded to an obvious need with imagination and creativity. He understood what was involved, and he fully accepted the consequences.

Finally, he knew himself. He had a grasp of his talents and weaknesses and how they fit in with those of his opponents. Thus, what he could not possibly have accomplished through military force or physical violence, he did through bravado, intimidation, and illusion. Any other tactics would have met with crushing defeat. This is not to imply that leaders should always behave in this manner. It simply suggests that these strategies employed by Wallenberg were essential to fulfill his objective under the most extraordinary of conditions and that they were chosen with full comprehension of the alternatives and their consequences.

In essence, the Wallenberg Effect suggests that becoming a mature leader means first becoming yourself, learning who you are and what you stand for. Implicit in this notion is the theory of self-discovery, getting in touch with oneself. Wallenberg teaches us that to grow as a leader involves reflecting on oneself, putting values in perspective, thinking about the task to be accomplished and influencing others to get the job done. Wallenberg's work in Hungary is a testimony that leaders are foot soldiers who battle for the ideals in which they believe and that leadership has far less to do with using other people than with serving other people. Plato said that "man is a being in search of meaning." In essence, servanthood is the key to successful leadership, which in turn can result in meaningful accomplishments. Raoul Wallenberg found himself and the meaning of his life by losing it in the service of others.

The process of learning about oneself and others, on an in-depth level, requires hard work. It is not something that can be gained solely from book study. It evolves best through personal introspection, human interaction and feedback, and through life experiences, observations, and analysis. It involves large quantities of common sense and realistic perspective. But its yield is high; it pays big dividends to those leaders who spend the time and make the extra effort to go beneath the surface, to discover what makes a person tick, because life and its activities are all part of the human experience. At bottom, it is all a matter of people, and the leader who understands people is prepared to win.

2. Objective

Every leader must have a clear, specific objective in mind at all times, a destination toward which all actions are directed. When the leader says forward march, everyone must know where forward is. If the leader lacks a sense of direction, then the followers will wind up some distance from the goal, like explorers without a compass or a guiding star.

Closely related to objective is vision, which implies having an acute sense of the possible. All effective leaders possess this capacity; they are able to focus sharply on what is to be done, seeing the objective as if through a powerful telescope.

Wallenberg exemplifies the principle that a clearly defined objective is absolutely essential as the focal point of our energies. His work in Hungary suggests that effective leadership is not neutral nor sterile but deeply emotional and that leaders must hold a sense of mission, a deeply felt belief in the worth of their objective. Nothing less has the necessary power to motivate leaders or followers to stretch the limits of their abilities. Total commitment comes only from total conviction that the goal is significant and right.

This ethical sense of mission grows out of a lifetime of value-building study and experience. However, the Wallenberg experience teaches us that much can be done in a short amount of time to impart principles upon which a given objective is based. All leaders should study the great foundational works of their nation to learn of the struggles of prior generations, ponder them, make them part of their being, determine how they apply to the situation at hand, and then transmit key principles to followers. History and philosophy form the underpinnings of the way of life for which people live and die. If values are thought to be only relative, if there is no right and wrong, if one system of government is morally equivalent to all others, then there is nothing worth sacrificing for. The leader will be limited to appeals to local pride and self-interest in attempting to inspire excellence. The result will often be halfhearted effort–and failure.

3. Ingenuity

Where only unquestioning obedience is valued, and where only strict adherence to rigid procedures is allowed, inflexibility and predictability are the consequences. But to succeed as a leader, or even to survive in a constantly changing and dangerous environment, creativity and adaptability are essential. This is where leaders must apply their foundational knowledge to the objective at hand and develop solutions, even in situations where there is no textbook answer.

Wallenberg knew that he had virtually no tangible resources and few allies. He also knew the type of people who stood in his path. And so, out of scraps of paper and a surplus of courage and personal character, he intimidated and defeated seemingly invincible enemies, time and again. Nazi numerical superiority and force of arms were powerless when confronted with a man who knew their own game better than they did and who could think faster than they could.

Throughout his entire experience in Hungary, in all that he did, Wallenberg had the daring to accept himself as a bundle of possibilities, and he boldly undertook the game of making the most of his best. Wallenberg instructs us that the leader is not a superman but is simply a fully functioning human being. Successful leaders are aware of their possibilities. Erich Fromm said that the pity in life today is that most of us die before we are fully born. Leaders such as Wallenberg are not merely observers of life, but active participants. They take the calculated risks required in exercising leadership and experimenting with the untried. It is surprising (and most aspiring leaders do not realize it) but much failure comes from people literally standing in their own way, preventing their own progress. Wallenberg never blocked his own path; rather, he created new paths where others saw only impenetrable walls. And in the process he was able to motivate others to do the same. He was a dispenser of hope in an environment filled with hopelessness and despair.

History is replete with instances where small, militarily weaker forces triumphed on the strength of superior strategy and tactics. Ingenuity makes surprise possible and allows quick adaptation and reaction to an adversary's actions. Without flexibility, humans are reduced to automatons, programmed only for failure.

Ingenuity requires information as its fuel. The established objective and the available tools and procedures provide the raw material for any leadership action. But much can be accomplished when leaders reach beyond traditional methods and use the status quo as a floor rather than a ceiling. Leaders must be evaluated on the basis of what they achieve. Results are what counts, not formulaic adherence to precedent. Wallenberg was an achiever; he was results-oriented. We, like him, can "do more with less" when we think creatively and are not confined to what has already been done. Military leaders are often criticized for preparing to fight the previous war. The best leaders think of all the possible ways in which available resources might be used or modified to achieve the objective as well as how the opposition might do the same. Who would have thought, for example, that silicon, common sand, would be the basis for the phenomenon of microcomputer chips and would revolutionize modern society? To see each problem from multiple perspectives is to multiply the possible solutions and open the door for victories that would be inconceivable under "conventional wisdom."

4. Confidence

Leaders create an environment in which ideas can flourish and see the light of day. To do this, leaders must be self-confident and have faith in themselves and others. People in leadership positions need a solid sense of self. It serves them well in times of turmoil, which inevitably await those who aspire to lead. The way people feel about themselves affects virtually every aspect of their lives. Self-esteem, which emerges from a sense of confidence, thus becomes the key to success or failure. In effect, leaders such as Wallenberg defy the law of averages and win because they expect success from themselves.

An indispensable ingredient of Wallenberg's success was an almost tangible self-confidence. He radiated certainty, composure, and authority, and this breathed life into his otherwise foolhardy actions. He compelled his enemies to accept as valid passports things such as library cards, laundry tickets, and even nothing at all. . .and he did it by infusing all of his actions with the sheer power of his personality. Through his aura of conviction, he also inspired people who, in many cases, had already resigned themselves to execution to join in his actions and save themselves and others.

Some would argue that the elusive quality we call "charisma" is a gift with which some people are blessed from birth. But, even if this is true, everyone can cultivate a positive attitude and an air of self-confidence within the bounds of his or her own personality.

This unique aspect of leadership tends to develop as a natural consequence from the qualities previously discussed. As leaders learn about themselves and their opposition, they identify their respective strengths and weaknesses and compose a creative strategy for bringing their own greatest assets to bear against their opponents' most vulnerable areas. Wallenberg understood, as did Napoleon, that "strategy is a simple art, it is just a matter of execution." When leaders act from a position of advantage, they feel confident that they will prevail . . . and this confidence will be perceived by friends and foes alike.

Leaders' actions will furthermore be focused on a purpose they believe to be right. This sense of the righteousness of the cause will also strengthen resolve. Conversely, where the leaders do not believe in the virtue of their actions, they will lack commitment and will be hindered by self-doubt. Such uncertainty will be apparent to others, undermining the confidence of followers and encouraging their opponents. It will contribute to eventual defeat and failure.

Wallenberg teaches us that it is important for each leader to become convinced of the worthiness of the mission, on some deeply felt level. Even when the immediate objective seems questionable, the leader must find justification in some indisputable value, such as support of the nation's honor. Then, that conviction must fortify all of the leader's actions. Wallenberg is a clear example that when a leader exudes a quiet confidence, surety, and decisiveness, followers will be inspired and opposition will be weakened. Leaders have been described as "strong," "powerful," "magnetic," and "charismatic." But, whatever else they may be, they certainly are self-confident, and from this confidence leaders are able to mobilize and inspire individuals and groups to make their own personal dreams and objectives come true.

5. Courage

When a sense of mission becomes powerful enough to motivate people to action, even in the face of personal danger or certain death, that is courage. To be courageous one need not be fearless; it is natural and good to be afraid when confronted with real risks. So long as that fear does not paralyze, there is courage at work.

Wallenberg knew he was entering a lion's den when he accepted his mission to Hungary. Innumerable times he ignored armed soldiers and even flying bullets to continue his rescue operations. He had the audacity to threaten high-ranking Nazi officers, who had proved their willingness to murder innocent civilians, let alone troublesome opponents, under conditions where they easily could have killed him. Although in constant fear for his life, he pressed on, risking and ultimately sacrificing himself for his mission.

Can courage be learned? It can, in the sense that the development of deep devotion to a cause galvanizes a person to act on behalf of that cause. This type of fundamental belief in the value of the mission is essential to the cultivation of courage.

If self-interest were the most important, then self-sacrifice would be out of the question. Only a profound conviction that there is a good greater than self can spark a person to risk everything for others. Self-sacrifice, and the courage to take that chance, are the antithesis of "me-generation" philosophy. When the lives or liberties of others are valued more highly than one's own life, then true courage can provide the fuel for remarkable accomplishments.

Wallenberg's life can help others form a series of constellations by which they can successfully chart their own contributions to humanity. A key element of what we call the Wallenberg Effect is this idea: Do not give in to life or its challenges. Dig in! Accept responsibility and in the process make a difference.

To some people, life is like the weather; it just happens to them. But to those who display the Wallenberg Effect (heroic leadership under adverse conditions) life is a great journey in human accomplishment. Wallenberg, like the trees of the Avenue of the Righteous, stands tall in the annals of man's "humanity" to man.

Few leaders will ever have the opportunity to help as many people as did Raoul Wallenberg. Still, each victory is immeasurably precious for those whose futures are spared. They, their children, their grandchildren, their entire posterity, and all whose lives will be touched by them, owe their existence to that one heartbeat of time when a person took action, despite the dangers. Although conditions may differ, the lessons for leadership that the Wallenberg Effect demonstrates should be valuable for all who aspire to more effective leadership. With patient application, it can be transferred and applied to everyday leadership problems, whether on the level of nations or individuals. As Wallenberg's medal testifies, *"Whoever saves a single soul, it is as if he had saved the whole world."*

The Wallenberg Effect on September 11

No discussion of courage as an element of leadership could be complete today without some mention of the events of September 11, 2001. In fact, the entirety of the Wallenberg Effect was very much in evidence in New York City, Washington DC, and many other places on that horrific day. We will focus on the passengers aboard United Flight 93, although there were numerous other outstanding feats of leadership on 9/11 and in its aftermath as well.

We will never know all the details of what happened on that aircraft in the brief time between takeoff and its ultimate crash in Pennsylvania. But it is apparent from analysis of the cockpit recorder and various in-flight telephone conversations that something remarkable transpired–something that showed the Wallenberg Effect in action and in full flower.

The passengers of Flight 93 at first had no more reason to suspect that the terrorists who commandeered their flight were bound for mass suicide than did the people on the other three doomed aircraft that morning. Common sense, rationality, and knowledge of previous hijackings over the years told them that these men would make demands, hold hostages, and eventually land the plane safely, somewhere, followed by a release of the hostages once their demands were met. In other words, there was initially no reason to panic, no cause to take drastic action.

But, as some of the passengers used their cell phones to call loved ones, the shocking news of the crashes into the Twin Towers of American Flight 11 and United Flight 175 reached the people on Flight 93. With breathtaking swiftness, a handful of passengers (1) learned the fate of the other planes, (2) deduced that their plane was headed for a similar end, (3) decided that they needed to do whatever they could to foil the terrorists' plot, (4) formulated a workable plan of action, (5) organized a capable team ready to execute their plan and (6) carried out their plan.

The terrorists had devoted months, perhaps years, to plotting, planning, and preparing for their deadly mission. All of this was utterly overwhelmed by a few ordinary American civilians in a matter of minutes because they knew what real leadership is all about.

Flight attendants readied coffee pots filled with boiling hot water to throw into the terrorists' faces. Passengers determined how to use fire extinguishers as weapons. They evaluated the abilities of the people available to them in light of the opponents they faced and decided who would do what when. Within the severe confines of an airline cabin, with narrow aisles and little room to maneuver, they calculated the best way to attack their foes. And then, they did it.

They did it on command. They did it when they heard the deathless words of passenger, husband, father, and hero Todd Beamer: "Let's roll!"

What would have happened if these people of Flight 93 had not taken action? It appears very likely that the terrorists would have crashed the aircraft into a major target in Washington, DC, just as American Flight 77 had devastated the Pentagon. The White House or the United States Capitol Building, and everyone in them, are the obvious targets that would have been there for the terrorists' taking. But the Wallenberg Effect—knowledge, objective, ingenuity, confidence, and courage—sparked the people of Flight 93 to sacrifice their own precious lives for the greater good. And they did it all within a few minutes, with virtually no physical resources, against a team of armed, determined, well prepared, professionally trained killers.

The key factor that made the difference for the people of Flight 93, and the many others who were saved through their heroism, was knowledge. Unlike the passengers on the first three ill-fated aircraft that day, they knew about the others in just enough time to do something about it. The result is an example of true leadership in action that should be told and retold forever. Raoul Wallenberg lives on in such people as the passengers of Flight 93 and in their legacy.

Discussion Questions and Ideas

- What do you think motivated Wallenberg, a wealthy, young, non-Jewish civilian citizen of neutral Sweden, to risk his life for the endangered Hungarian Jews? What motivates you in the duties you perform? Why are you in the occupation you now pursue?

- What enabled Wallenberg to inspire, in those he helped, a belief in the possibility of success and a willingness to try in the face of hopelessness and resignation to defeat? Have you ever known leaders who could cause positive transformations in the attitude of the people under their care? How did they accomplish this? What effect have you had on the attitude of the people you lead? Why?

• How could Wallenberg, who had no weapons and little if any official status or power in Nazi-occupied Hungary, induce his Nazi and Arrow Cross enemies, including their highest ranking officers, to do his bidding? Have you ever faced a situation in which you had to "do more with less" and tackle a problem with seemingly inadequate resources? What did you do? What were the results?

• Was it morally wrong for Wallenberg to use deception, threats, and bribery in furtherance of his mission? Compare and contrast his situation with examples from your experience in which you were tempted to "bend the rules."

• Consider the following two sentences. Which comes closer to your own personal view? Why? For what, if anything, would you be willing to risk your life? Why?

"Nothing is worth dying for."

"If nothing is worth dying for, nothing is worth living for."

- How would you define the word "hero?" What qualities or feats constitute heroism? Have you known anyone you consider to be a hero? To what extent is heroism important to your life and career?

- How do you identify potential leaders? What sets leaders apart from other members of an organization?

- How can you incorporate the Wallenberg Effect into your work and your life?

- How would you rate Wallenberg as a leader? Why?

- How did the people of Flight 93 exemplify each of the aspects of the Wallenberg Effect?

- How could a group of strangers on Flight 93 accomplish all that they did so quickly, with no advance planning and almost no physical resources, when faced with a well-prepared, armed group of professional killers determined to use their aircraft as a missile? Or, in some way, did these passengers have advance preparation for September 11?

- What would you have done if you had been on Flight 93?

- If you had been on Flight 93, what would you have done with the short time available to make one last phone call?

Bibliography and Recommended Reading

Anger, P. *With Raoul Wallenberg in Budapest.* New York: Holocaust Library, 1981.

Bennis, W. *On Becoming a Leader.* Reading, MA: Addison-Wesley, 1989.

Bennis, W. and B. Nanus. *Leaders: The Strategies for Taking Charge.* New York: Harper and Row, 1985.

Bierman, J. *Righteous Gentile.* New York: Viking Press, 1981.

Greenleaf, R. *Servant Leadership.* New York: Paulist Press, 1981.

Hersey, P. and K. Blanchard. *Management of Organizational Behavior.* Englewood Cliffs, NJ: Prentice-Hall, 1988.

Human Rights in Eastern Europe and the Soviet Union. Committee on Foreign Affairs

Lester, E. *Wallenberg: The Man in the Iron Web.* New Jersey: Prentice-Hall, 1982.

Lester, R., exec. ed. *Concepts for Air Force Leadership* (AU-24). Montgomery, AL: Air University Press, 1990.

Marton, K. *Wallenberg.* New York: Random House, 1982.

Peters, T. *Thriving on Chaos.* New York: Knopf, 1987.

Rosenfeld, H. *Raoul Wallenberg, Angel of Rescue.* Buffalo: Prometheus Books, 1982.

Werbell, F. and T. Clarke. *Lost Hero: The Mystery of Raoul Wallenberg.* New York: McGraw-Hill, 1982.

Zalenznik, A. *The Leadership Gap.* The Washington Quarterly, 1983 and Subcommittee on International Organizations,

House of Representatives, Ninety-Sixth

Congress. Washington: U.S. GPO, 1980.

Chapter 4

Leadership and the Art of Mentoring

Executive Summary

Mentoring is both an opportunity and a risk. It is largely a teaching process beginning with parental nurturing of children and continuing through the lifecycle of organizational and personal interrelationships. A key principle considered in this chapter is that mentoring is both an obligation and responsibility of leadership. Through mentoring, the wisdom and experience of the senior is passed to the junior. This includes passing on and discussing principles, traditions, shared values, quality, and lessons learned. Mentoring provides a framework to bring about a cultural change in the way we view the professional development of competent future leaders. The road to the top in most organizations today is an uphill and bumpy ride–you cannot simply float to the top. Mentoring is a key tool to help us get to our destination.

Discussion

Mentoring is perhaps the most powerful method by which we can shape the future. The term has become a buzzword, often carelessly shot into the air along with a dust cloud of other jargon, from the unofficial, unwritten dictionary of those who consider themselves the cutting edge of modern leadership and management. But real mentoring, properly understood, is much more than just another clipping from last week's Dilbert cartoon. Without an in-depth study of mentoring, the capacity of individuals to mentor is limited to the horizons of their own experience. Thus, mentoring is literally a time machine that allows us to have a profound influence many years beyond today's hubbub and humdrum. And, it is safe to say that, just as sure as you are related to your grandfather, mentoring can make a significant difference in the lives of people.

A mentor is a trusted advisor, teacher, counselor, friend, and/or parent, older and more senior than the person he or she helps. Mentors are there when you need them. Mentoring is an ongoing process. In organizations, it can apply to all leaders and supervisors who are responsible for getting their work done through other people. The individual who is assisted by a mentor is usually called a protégé–in essence, a student or pupil who learns from the mentor. The process by which one person aids another in this type of relationship is known as "mentoring." Regardless of how we choose to define it, mentoring–if properly conducted–can have a most positive change in the life, attitudes, and behavior of the protégé. But what does this really mean? Does mentoring differ in any way from teaching, parenting, or being a friend?

This chapter attempts to answer these important questions in a practical way that will enable people to implement the principles of mentoring in everyday life. If we comprehend the principles essential to mentoring, we will have in our grasp the tool kit that can make our time machine work. On balance, this chapter attempts to demystify the phenomenon of mentoring by cutting through buzzwords and misconceptions to communicate a workable understanding of mentoring and its practical implementation.

The Mentoring Process

It may be a useful mnemonic and analytical device to treat the term mentoring as if it were an acronym. The various aspects of effective mentoring, expressed as verbs, can be understood as corresponding to the letters in the word as follows:

> **M**odel
> **E**mpathize
> **N**urture
> **T**each
> **O**rganize
> **R**espond
> **I**nspire
> **N**etwork
> **G**oal-set

We will discuss each of the components in turn and, in so doing, will develop a working understanding of what it means to be a mentor.

Model

An effective mentor must lead by example. When the mentor serves as a real-world role model for the protégé, the cliché that "actions speak louder than words" comes to life.

Mentoring requires significant amounts of time for mentor and protégé to be in close proximity. The protégé is always observing and learning from the mentor. The opportunity to see how the mentor actually deals with a variety of situations is an important part of the process because it takes things from the abstract, conceptual level to the realm of practical, pragmatic application.

A mentor must behave at all times, both publicly and privately, as if the protégé were the mentor's shadow. Part of the mentoring process is the act of demonstrating for the protégé as he or she "shadows" the mentor the proper methods, techniques, practices, and procedures that are part of the way the enterprise functions. More than this, though, is the need for the mentor to show the protégé how a mature professional deals with various challenges and opportunities. A mentor should be a model of composure, dignity, integrity, and professionalism, under all manner of conditions. A protégé who shadows such a role model will eventually come to understand, at a deep level, what he or she must be and do. A successful protégé is one who is willing to listen, observe, learn, and grow from the example of another.

An outstanding mentor who personified the principle of modeling ideal behavior was the great baseball player and Hall of Famer, Jackie Roosevelt Robinson. It may be hard to believe for people who grew up after the dawning of the Civil Rights movement, but until 1947 almost all "major league" professional sports in America were completely closed to African-Americans. No matter how talented, even the best African-American athletes could never play in the all-white professional leagues. But in 1947, Jackie Robinson bravely broke the "color barrier" and became a major league baseball player for the Brooklyn Dodgers.

It was a very tough challenge for Robinson. He had to overcome bitter, angry resistance, and resentment from some of his own teammates, let alone opposing players, managers, and owners. He was repeatedly subjected to the most vile racial slurs, obscenities, and insults. Players would intentionally try to injure him with their spiked shoes as they slid into him at his position at second base. In some cities, he could not eat in the same restaurants as his teammates, nor sleep in the same hotels. It was a hard, lonely struggle for this young man—the one and only African-American in all of major league baseball. But Jackie Robinson was prepared. He understood and applied the four Ps: preparation prevents poor performance.

Dodgers owner Branch Rickey had met with Robinson prior to the season to discuss the risks they were both taking and the difficulties they were certain to encounter. They agreed that it was crucial for Robinson not to sink to the level of his attackers. Bigots would be circling constantly like vultures, all too eager to pounce on any excuse to find Robinson somehow "unfit" for the major leagues. In their view, if Robinson proved unfit, then by extension so did all other African-Americans. Jackie Robinson represented an entire race, and he would be under intense scrutiny at all times. The pressure was crushing and unrelenting, but Robinson never let it beat him.

Every day, he played all-star caliber baseball on the field. He also conducted himself like the consummate professional and gentleman he was, both on and off the field. He carried himself with quiet dignity notwithstanding the most brutal indignities thrown at him. The only way he fought back was by playing baseball with an unsurpassed degree of dedication, drive, energy, and determination, game after game. In so doing, he gradually won the grudging respect of many former enemies and demonstrated for countless other African-Americans that there was hope for them too. To this day, he remains a shining role model for everyone who must deal with racism and discrimination of whatever variety.

In time, Jackie personally mentored other African-American baseball players who entered the major leagues through the doors he had opened, including teammates Roy Campanella and Don Newcombe. He told them what they needed to know, and, more importantly, he showed them. His example proved to them, on a daily basis, what was needed to succeed. Because of his influence, it was easier for them and for everyone else who came later. He was the model for them to emulate, personally and professionally. That is what mentors do.

Clearly, lessons of this type do not lend themselves to a quick one-time demonstration. This is not an easy, by-the-numbers, single-shot process. A person becomes a mentor and a role model through persistent effort and interaction with the protégé over a considerable period of time. It may be that a mentor can teach the basics of a task at hand fairly quickly, but the deeper lessons that distinguish mentoring from simply teaching or training require prolonged involvement. You cannot model optimal actions over a broad spectrum of conditions at once, at will; it must happen naturally, in its own time. With enough time, and given a sufficiently wide range of circumstances, a relationship can mature from one of trainer-trainee to the more transformational one of mentor-protégé. An effective mentor is like an elephant that tramples down high grass and flattens bushes to ease the way for the younger, quicker animals. Real mentors exhibit caring for others. They are inspirational and high-minded, with tremendous energy and a positive attitude toward making a difference in people's lives. This requires that a mentor be capable of maintaining a give-and-take relationship with a protégé. In turn, protégés must be willing to learn, actively seek help, and apply what they have learned.

Empathize

The ability and willingness to empathize are central to mentoring. Only by truly understanding what the protégé is experiencing and by identifying with what the protégé is feeling, can the mentor know what is needed. Without empathy, the would-be mentor is reduced to acting in a canned, off-the-shelf, generic, one-size-fits-all manner, and the protégé is robbed of the individualized focus that is so important to every mentoring relationship.

Mentoring involves something more than teaching. This extra ingredient is empathy, a measure of interpersonal involvement and caring. In fact, empathy is in many respects the Golden Rule in practice—we treat others as we would like them to treat us in similar circumstances.

An empathic mentor will comprehend the types of challenges and struggles a novice faces, usually because he or she was once a novice too. It may take a little jog around the memory track to recollect those long-suppressed thoughts of the painful early days, but it is worth the effort. A mentor who remembers what it is like to be new and inexperienced will be far more effective in assisting others in that position.

When a mentor puts himself or herself in the protégé's stiff, squeaky new shoes, he or she knows without being told which areas are likely to be causing discomfort and difficulties. The mentor can anticipate problems and needs and proactively take steps to smooth the path. The protégé will appreciate this because it saves asking countless questions. It shows consideration for the protégé's need for self-respect. Empathy helps form a bond between mentor and protégé, thereby, fostering the kind of mutual commitment that characterizes mentoring at its best.

One of the most remarkable mentors in history is Anne Sullivan, the teacher of Helen Keller. Immortalized in the play and film *The Miracle Worker,* Sullivan exemplified all facets of an ideal mentor as she worked with her young deaf and blind protégé. Perhaps most notable, however, was her steadfast determination to empathize with her very challenging student. Sullivan had to overcome multiple daunting obstacles—a seven-year old, "spoiled," wildly undisciplined, extremely stubborn Helen Keller, who almost from birth had been unable to see or hear! How would she ever be able to connect with such a pupil? How could she hope to teach her anything at all? Virtually all of the usual teaching methods were utterly useless.

Anne could not teach her student by pointing to objects or by showing her words and pictures in a conventional book because Helen was unable to see. She could not teach by reading aloud or explaining things orally because Helen was unable to hear. Each of these conditions alone would have been formidable obstacles, but together they made the situation virtually impossible. Plus, Helen was so young and had been encased in sightlessness and silence since such an early stage of her infancy that she had no preexisting knowledge of or experience with any form of alternate communication method or language.

Anne Sullivan is known the world over as the miracle worker because she did indeed overcome all these obstacles and succeeded in teaching Helen to an astonishing degree. Helen's parents would have been thrilled if she had learned even to sit at the dinner table without becoming violent. Ultimately, Sullivan took Helen far beyond that first hurdle and taught her to read and write to such a phenomenal level that Helen graduated from prestigious Radcliffe College and became a famous author. Sullivan accomplished this monumental achievement largely because she tenaciously refused to admit defeat and gradually attained true empathy with Helen.

Fortified with a powerful determination to comprehend the world as Helen knew it and drawing deeply from her own experiences to make every possible analogy, Sullivan burrowed through the multiple walls imprisoning her pupil. With tremendous persistence, she vicariously entered the dark, strange, silent world of her protégé and developed a combination of techniques that would penetrate all those layers of separation between them. Once she achieved the initial breakthrough, Helen's indomitable spirit burst forth in an exultant tidal wave of freedom and carried both mentor and protégé to undreamed-of heights. Helen eventually summarized her experiences as Anne Sullivan's protégé in these words: "It was the birthday of my soul, the day my teacher came to me."

It is useful to keep this example in mind. The Golden Rule is a superb guiding principle for all mentors. Empathize with your protégé, and treat him or her as you would want to be treated. Comprehend not merely the person's position but actual circumstances. As Anne Sullivan has shown, this is the key to building bridges across even the widest chasms.

Nurture

Nurturing encompasses a caring attitude, with an emphasis on development, and an understanding of the "law of the harvest." The mentor nurtures the protégé as a farmer tends the wheat, providing seeds, nourishment, protection, and the room to grow, each in its turn, in the proper amount, and in its own due time.

Most significant is that harvesting is a natural process that abides by certain unchanging principles, in a definite sequence. No farmer can reap before sowing nor expect a rich harvest without a sizable prior investment of time, talent, and labor. These seem to be obvious points, but they are often missed by people who are "too busy" to do more than go through the motions of mentoring.

If mentoring is to be more than a mirage, if it is to be a real process rather than illusory window-dressing, the mentor will have to tend to the real needs of the protégé. Seeds of knowledge must be planted and watered, cultivated with sufficient tools (and the information necessary to use them properly), and given enough time for the seeds to germinate and take root. Only later can the crop be weeded and given more advanced nutrients. Then still more time must be allowed before any harvest is expected. It is impossible for a farmer to receive on-demand a bounteous harvest according to some artificially imposed "schedule" if the seedlings have been denied the time to mature and bear ripened fruit. This is the law of the harvest. Its components and its sequence are established by nature and are forever immutable.

To nurture a human being, similar natural laws must be obeyed. We cannot reasonably expect a harvest of expert-level performance from someone who has not had the appropriate training or the time to apply and internalize that training through actual trial and error. Not only is it unrealistic, but it is also extremely frustrating to the person who is placed into such an unfair situation. Similarly, it is not enough to give a trainee a computer, or any other tool, if we fail to provide the necessary practical instruction on how to use it effectively.

On a more intangible level, nurturing requires the mentor to care about, and to care for, the protégé. This, too, cannot be faked or rushed or forced. If the mentor is unwilling to learn what motivates the protégé and to develop a degree of co-ownership of their aspirations, there will be a lack of nurturing.

A fascinating example of the nurturing aspect of mentoring comes from the world of literature. Don Quixote, the odd, visionary, self-made "knight" created by the brilliant Spanish novelist Miguel de Cervantes, has been amusing and amazing people for hundreds of years. In both the classic novel and in the more recent musical play and film *Man of La Mancha,* Don Quixote touched the life of a troubled young prostitute named Aldonza.

Many people who met the highly eccentric old man assumed that he was insane. Here, after all, was a fellow riding around Spain as a knight-errant long after knights in armor had passed from the scene, doing battle with windmills he imagined to be menacing giants. Don Quixote saw everything as grander and more magical than it appeared to "sane" folks, including his cherished "golden helmet," which others saw as an ordinary barber's basin.

This applied to the people Don Quixote met, too. He saw in the simple peasant Sancho Panza the makings of a noble squire to assist him in his knightly missions. He saw in the rough, bitter, cynical prostitute Aldonza a wonderful, virtuous lady of the highest principles to whom he would dedicate his greatest victories. To him, she even had a loftier, sweeter, more musical name–Dulcinea. Through many adventures, he consistently treated Sancho and Aldonza as if they truly were the people he envisioned them to be.

Aldonza, in particular, fought him on this every step of the way. Years of abuse, degradation, and poverty had taught her that life was miserable and she was worthless. But Don Quixote steadfastly treated her as the fine lady of nobility, Dulcinea, in public and in private and in all manner of circumstances. He was totally dedicated to serving her, defending her honor, and building her up. With complete consistency, he behaved as if she were the royal lady of his dreams. And very gradually this patient nurturing began to have an effect.

People usually are not transformed overnight. The law of the harvest says that things happen in their natural order, with the time they naturally require, and not one minute less. On some level, Don Quixote knew this, and he persisted in nurturing Aldonza despite her many angry refusals to be helped. Eventually, the harvest did come, and she became a different, better person. At the conclusion of the musical play, she even declares, "My name is Dulcinea." Such is the power of a mentor who nurtures not just for a day, and not just when it is convenient or easy to do so, but with dedication and long-term commitment.

There is a difference between nurturing someone and being a mother hen. Good parents must let their children make some of their own decisions, including the inevitable mistakes, and learn to deal with the consequences. Through grappling with gradually increasing degrees of autonomy and living with the natural aftershocks of bad decisions, children eventually become responsible adults who gain independence from their parents. So, too, must good mentors allow their protégés progressively increasing degrees of independence, together with the concomitant responsibility for their actions.

Any attempt to shelter people from all painful experiences will fail. No greenhouse environment, no matter how carefully constructed, can artificially protect its inhabitants—whether beans or human beings—indefinitely. Even if it could be done, the result would be people incapable of functioning as independent individuals in the real world. The key to effective nurturing is to maintain a balance between protecting the protégé and weaning them away from dependence. This is an imprecise process that requires mentors continually to monitor their protégés' progress and make the necessary adjustments. It does not lend itself to rigid timetables or cookbook recipes. Only an actively engaged mentor can know his or her protégé well enough to gauge the appropriate mix of sheltering and weaning.

Teach

A central aspect of mentoring is the process of teaching. Mentors teach their protégés, first and foremost. Indeed, teaching in its fullest, most developed sense is the essence of mentoring.

Many people, no matter how knowledgeable and experienced, are uncomfortable with teaching others. They often have had no training as teachers. They may have been trained by ineffective teachers themselves and assume that the methods that were used to teach them are appropriate for them now to use on others. They may have little interest in being a teacher, or they may not comprehend how the concepts that are so familiar and second nature to them are foreign, difficult, and time-consuming for a novice to grasp.

There are many theories of education, each with their champions and critics. It is beyond the scope of this chapter to examine educational theory in depth. For our purposes, it will suffice to note that there is substantial evidence that by far the most effective teaching method, across the entire spectrum of subjects, is a common-sense approach known as direct instruction. For both short-term and long-term learning, in categories from mathematics to reading to logical reasoning, direct instruction has been shown to be a very powerful teaching method.

Developed by Siegfried Engelmann, direct instruction relies on time-tested methods that seem obvious but are very often neglected by amateur and professional teachers alike. In essence, the best results come from teachers who: (1) organize the material into logical, step-by-step, building-block units of manageable size; (2) correct students' errors immediately; (3) frequently review all previously covered material and relate it to the current lesson; (4) include generous amounts of practical exercises on which students can flex their developing intellectual muscles; and (5) often test students' comprehension, formally and informally, and give them detailed feedback on their progress. With these basic principles constantly in mind, anyone can be an effective teacher.

It is crucial for mentors to spend some time developing a realistic plan for teaching their protégés. This requires empathy in that the expert mentor must put himself or herself in the place of the novice protégé and determine what information needs to be conveyed, in what sequence, over what period of time. The mentor must realize that this material is totally new to the novice and that most people need to see or hear unfamiliar material several times before they truly learn it. A one-time explanation is not enough, particularly when there is a great deal of material involved.

People differ in the ways they learn most readily. Some people learn by reading, so the mentor must provide a written set of resources to the protégé, complete with instructions on where to look for further help. Some learn by watching others perform the task in question, so the mentor must model the appropriate behavior. Other people learn by listening, so the mentor must also methodically, thoroughly, and with repetition talk the protégé through each concept. Still other people learn by doing, armed with a basic overview of the material. Thus, every effective training program will include ample practical exercises in which the trainees have the opportunity to test and expand their knowledge of previously presented oral and written material. These exercises must be done with the mentor's participation to correct errors swiftly, offer helpful tips, and answer questions as they arise.

Because people vary in how they learn, it is a good idea to use all of the above methods, in combination, with any given protégé. At least until and unless it becomes clear that a person finds some methods far more effective than others, a mentor should provide a mixture of all of these approaches (reading, shadowing, listening, and doing) to give the protégé the best possible chance to learn.

Teaching must also progress in a logical, building-block manner. Mentors should begin by thoroughly establishing a solid foundation of the simplest, most general concepts and skills. These must include understandable definitions of all terms and acronyms, which often are used so profusely by experienced people that they fail to realize that others are unfamiliar with the vocabulary of this strange new language. It is a good idea to provide a written handout that defines all the key terms and acronyms in layman's verbiage.

Only when satisfied that the protégé has a firm grasp of the basics can the mentor build upon this foundation and add the next layer of complexity. It is very easy for unskilled teachers to get off track and jump erratically from concept to concept, but that spells disaster for the learning process. This happens because the mentor knows so much more about the topic than the protégé, and his or her brain automatically fills in all the gaps in the subject matter. By empathizing with the protégé and organizing a plan of action, the mentor should be able to determine which concepts depend on a foundation of basic knowledge and to teach both basic and advanced topics without skipping around and leaving gapping holes in the lessons.

Socrates, the great teacher and philosopher of ancient Greece, made a very powerful teaching tool famous. Socrates would ask questions of his students, including Plato, and through their answers and his skillful use of follow-up questions, he led them to think through the material for themselves. Day after day, the streets of Athens were the stage for this remarkable, interactive learning process. Plato became an immortal philosopher in his own right under the expert tutelage of his mentor Socrates, and later, in turn, Plato mentored another great thinker, Aristotle, who then mentored Alexander the Great. Such is the nature of mentoring, as one generation learns from the preceding mentors and then teaches the succeeding generation. Through his influence on his illustrious followers, Socrates profoundly affected the course of Western civilization.

This so-called Socratic method of questions and answers is a very effective way to teach. It is often used in law schools today, as it has been for many decades, because it causes students to learn a new *way of thinking*, not merely new information. It compels both teacher and student to be involved and actively engaged in the educational process. There is no room for passivity when there is a continual interchange of ideas, questions, and responses. The stereotype of the traditional lecture-dominated classroom populated with near-comatose students lulled to sleep by a droning bore of a teacher is the antithesis of a lively, stimulating Socratic dialogue.

Mentors should incorporate this technique of periodically asking their protégés questions and, based on their answers, assessing the need for either additional questions or further instruction. This is an excellent way to test a student's progress, quickly, frequently, and informally, and provide crucial early warning of problem areas that require more attention from the mentor. As Engelmann notes, "If the student hasn't learned, the material hasn't been taught." If a student can thoroughly explain the material to the teacher, in the student's own words, that is strong evidence that the material has, in fact, been taught and learned.

It is also absolutely essential that the mentor periodically review previously presented material with the protégé. All successful teaching programs include frequent reviews of previous lessons with logical ties to the areas currently being studied. Repetition is an important component of learning, and the mentor simply has to take this into account. Again, it is all too easy to forget to conduct reviews or to assume that they are unnecessary. If the lesson is important enough to present the first time, it is important enough to review. If it is not reviewed, there is a high probability that it will not be learned. Remember, people internalize new information best when the material is presented in multiple ways (reading, observing, hearing, and doing) and at multiple times (reviewing). In instructional terms, what is required are real events, initiatives, and experiences capable of changing the mentoring trajectory, i.e., making mentoring more central to the ever-increasing role of the leader as a teacher. Keep it simple, keep it practical, and ensure that leaders are doing the actual teaching. The teaching purpose of mentoring should be cultural, rather than structural; personal development is the first priority–the kind that produces enhanced knowledge of attitudes and results in new and improved behaviors. Credibility and competence are the two essential things that protégés are looking for in this aspect of mentoring.

Organize

A mentor must be organized to be of much help to the protégé and must also help the protégé become organized. The systematic, methodical approach is essential, both in preparing an effective mentoring program and in building the protégé into a more effective individual.

An organized mentor will know at the outset what he or she wants to achieve and will focus every aspect of the program toward that goal. As the saying goes: "If you don't know where you're going, how will you know when you get there?" By developing a desired-end state before beginning the mentoring process, a mentor gains the ability to gear every effort in that direction. Organization and planning are a vital part of a good teaching program. The time and effort spent organizing thoughts and materials into a logical, building-block, sequential plan of lessons all aimed at a definite, precisely defined target of what needs to be learned will pay big dividends in the form of improved learning and the quicker, better performance that follows.

Some people claim to have no patience for the organizing process. They would much rather "just do it" and skip the tedious preliminaries. They believe that because they are so experienced and intelligent it would be a waste of time for them to "go through the motions" of organizing a mentoring plan. They are mistaken.

Mentoring is too important a journey to commence without a prior investment of time and effort to develop an organized road map or plan of action. "Winging it" does not do it justice. No matter how much you know or how experienced you are, you still need to organize. In fact, paradoxically, it may be that the need for organization is greatest where a mentor is most knowledgeable and experienced because such an expert is more likely to take the basics for granted and omit key points. A person who is serious about being a mentor will spend the time to ensure that it is done properly. Mentoring is not a window-dressing, feel-good program to be given a cursory treatment and then forgotten once someone has given us credit for it on a monthly report. Mentoring involves real people and real commitments between them, on a continuing basis. It is worth the time spent to organize a coherent, individually tailored plan. Failure to organize will result in aimless drift–largely random activity–with no guiding principle to steer the ship toward any particular port.

Organizing may not be the most emotionally rewarding facet of mentoring or the most fun. People tend to prefer to spend their limited time actually interacting with protégés or engaged in other activities that feel more like action and less like paperwork. But, if you neglect to organize your efforts, you are unlikely to achieve the best results. In essence, the time you devote to organizing saves a lot of time and energy. It enables us to minimize or eliminate the resources we squander on irrelevant or secondary activities while focusing maximum attention on our real goal and the key stepping stones along the way.

One virtue of analyzing the mentoring process is to give our efforts structure, a workable framework within which to organize our thoughts and actions. A topic-by-topic breakdown of the important ingredients of the process provides a ready-made outline to keep us on track and aimed at our target. An outline compels us to examine the essential facets of an effective mentoring approach. It leads us to devote some time to planning a method of addressing each aspect of the mentoring process, armed with an understanding of what should be achieved. Similar to a good checklist, an outline provides some assurance that major components will not be inadvertently left out or given inadequate attention. This is all part and parcel of what it means to organize. It may not be exciting, but it is a key to success.

Finally, because one significant lesson all mentors should teach their protégés is organizational skill, it is necessary first for the mentor to learn and use this tool. As mentioned previously, a mentor must model the desired behavior.

Respond

Mentoring is a communicative process. It is not a method for shooting information at a person who writes down every word. The ideal mentor is not a guru perched motionless atop a remote Himalayan mountain peak, sitting with legs folded and navel in mind, dispensing wisdom periodically like a fortune-telling vending machine. Mentoring involves genuine two-way communication between mentor and protégé on a protracted, continuing basis.

Mentors must truly listen to questions from their protégés and respond to them fully. This requires active listening from protégés. Mentors should follow up with more questions after the initial question to ensure their protégés understand the answer and are satisfied with it. It is important to remember that the primary client or customer in any mentor-protégé relationship is the protégé. The protégé knows best when there are relationship problems, inadequately answered questions, or a pace that makes effective learning impossible. The mentor must respond to the protégé's needs if the mentoring process is to succeed.

Less obviously, but also very important, the mentor must respond to the protégé on multiple communication levels throughout the mentoring process. The protégé may be reluctant to voice certain concerns or to ask too many questions. An effective mentor must be alert for nonverbal indications and cues. It takes some diligence, sensitivity, and perceptiveness for a mentor to develop the capacity to respond to the protégé in this manner. A protégé who discovers the mentor is sufficiently in tune to respond even to unspoken questions and problems will be more likely to appreciate and to bond to that mentor.

A mentor should be available much of the time. Particularly in the early phases of a mentoring relationship, a mentor must be prepared to devote sizable amounts of time.

Although other duties will demand the mentor's time as well, a mentor has to be physically present and actively involved with the protégé if the process is to work. Many aspects of the mentoring process require frequent interaction and the continual exchange of information between mentor and protégé. It is impossible to "mail it in" and somehow rig up a shortcut around the day to day facets of mentoring. At best, any such attempt to do an end run around the requirement to be responsive would be a counterfeit facsimile of mentoring. It might bear some superficial similarities to mentoring, but it would lack the power and efficacy of the real thing.

Do not confuse responding with being reactive or sitting back waiting to answer questions. A responsive mentor does not merely react to a protégé but is proactive. Mentors must anticipate needs, problems, and concerns and try to take care of them in advance. This is one area where another key principle, organization, is particularly helpful. With proper organization, a mentor can foresee many of the usual pitfalls along the way and do as much as possible to build precautions against them into the mentoring plan.

Jaime Escalante demonstrated the principle of responsiveness in a most remarkable way, as memorialized in the film *Stand and Deliver.* He stunned his colleagues when he left his high paying position in the computer industry to become a mathematics teacher in a low-income Hispanic section of Los Angeles. What he found when he entered his classroom was a disheartened collection of underachieving, streetwise teenagers whose minds and hearts were on anything but mathematics. But Escalante was determined to use all of his considerable skills to make a difference for these young people, regardless of the cost to him personally in terms of time, effort, lost income, and frustration.

Escalante decided to teach his students calculus–not just high school mathematics–although many people would have considered even basic math an achievement in itself. To make this happen, he knew he had to respond to his class not as a class, and not as a cluster of stereotypes, but as unique individuals. He worked hard to explain calculus from the most basic principles, illustrating his points with real-life examples from his students' own experiences. He appealed to their ethnic pride by stressing the illustrious history of Hispanic achievement in higher mathematics, including the groundbreaking advancements of the ancient Mayans. And he tailored his teaching methods to the needs of each student. If that meant supplemental review sessions in his own home, over dinner, then that is exactly what he provided. Even after he suffered a serious heart attack, he refused to relax; his students needed him, and he was not about to let them down.

The results of Jaime Escalante's work were so phenomenal that they became the subject of a popular motion picture—hardly the place one would usually expect to find a high school calculus class! His inner-city students performed like superstars on the difficult Advanced Placement calculus examination and earned a huge head start on their college mathematics careers. Escalante repeated this feat year after year, mentoring ever-increasing numbers of students from his previously obscure school to reach unheard-of achievements in calculus. Moreover, his responsiveness to and total involvement with each student helped them in many aspects of their lives, not just in academics. Under his care, they proved to the world and to themselves that they could excel in any forum, against any odds. That is the impact of a mentor who responds to each protégé on a meaningful, individualized level.

Inspire

A mentor should be more than a good role model, teacher, and helpful acquaintance. Important though all of those are, true mentoring encompasses something extra, an element of inspiration. The mentor who can inspire the protégé will have a profound, deeply rooted effect on that person for perhaps an entire lifetime. When inspired, a person is powerfully motivated to transform himself or herself into something better than before. Inspiration is the key to the most fundamental, core-level transformations.

Inspiration is one way in which leaders differ from managers. A leader has a broader vision and a far-reaching drive that goes beyond the more limited focus on daily operations that is the typical province of managers. The best mentors will also be good leaders because similar qualities are required of both.

Can a person acquire the ability to inspire others? Are there steps a person can take to improve the chances of being an inspirational individual, a leader? To some extent, inspiration is a matter of chemistry and does not lend itself to conscious analysis or application use, but there are things a mentor can do to enhance this important element of the mentoring process.

It is useful to read about leadership, especially in-depth discussions of some inspirational leaders. Reading a few case studies of effective leaders will lend at least an intellectual understanding of some of the key factors that can form the foundation for more pragmatic, action-driving steps.

Probably the most significant factor contributing to one person's ability to inspire another is integrity. The mentor must have, and be perceived to have, integrity. No one is apt to be inspired by a hypocrite. We are moved by people we admire, and we admire people who exemplify qualities we want to have. Honesty, consistency, and commitment to correct principles are traits we can all strive to incorporate into our approach to life. Over time, with sufficient testing in stressful situations, these traits will add up to integrity and help us to inspire those who look to us for guidance.

The other central element of inspirational character is a selfless, altruistic nature. People who are willing to sacrifice their own self-interest for the good of others tend to inspire others. Altruism is a noble quality refreshingly different from the usual human tendency to ask "what's in it for me." We trust and admire people who have proven themselves to be unselfish and that naturally leads to our being inspired by their example.

Example, as usual, is crucial. Although a protégé might be inspired by the mentor's words, that will soon wear off if the mentor's actions fail to support what is said. No one needs to take a course in rhetoric or hire a professional speechwriter in order to be an inspiration. If the mentor is the type of person others might wish to emulate, and if the protégé has ample opportunities to observe the mentor handling difficult situations, the inspiration will follow.

A contemporary mentor who embodies the principle of inspiration is Marva Collins. This famous educator has taught generations of impoverished, disadvantaged, inner-city children from the roughest neighborhoods of Chicago. Collins has never been content just to achieve an orderly classroom, although many would consider that a major victory under the circumstances. Despite the discouraging predictions of hordes of self-styled educational experts, she has taught thousands of poverty level African-American children to read, write, compute, and achieve several grade levels above their age group. More than this, she has instilled in them a genuine love of Shakespeare, Dante, the Greek philosophers and many other things typically assumed to be far beyond the grasp of her young pupils. Under her guidance, African-American children as young as three or four years old learn to read, memorize and recite lengthy passages, and analyze sophisticated themes from the great thinkers of civilization. She has proven her maxim, "Any child can be a real achiever," thousands of times over.

Marva Collins is, of course, a master teacher. Her nononsense, low-budget, back-to-basics approach has worked wonders, especially when combined with her unconquerable faith in the worth of every child and her absolute refusal to accept failure from herself or her students. She has twice, twenty years apart, been featured in glowing reports on the television news magazine program *60 Minutes*. She has twice been formally invited by presidents of the United States to be Secretary of Education–invitations she declined because she did not want to leave her inner-city classroom. She is in constant demand as a speaker and is the author of several successful books. She has achieved her astonishing results, where so many others have failed, in large part because she knows how to inspire her very youthful protégés.

Her students see her every day working endlessly with total dedication and genuine love with each individual child no matter how difficult and resistant to change the child may be. They see her doing the same things she exhorts them to do, including reading and re-reading every book she assigns them. They see her, an African-American woman from a small town in Alabama, refusing to throw any "pity parties" for herself no matter how much prejudice and discrimination is thrown in her path. They see her devoting her time, talents, indeed everything she has, including her life savings, to Westside Preparatory and the other schools she has founded. They see her demanding the same lofty standards from herself that she expects from them–excellence and achievement, hard work and persistence. And they see that she never gives up on them, just as she tells them every day never to give up on themselves.

Day after day, Marva spends time with every student, one on one. She cradles a child's face lovingly in her hands, looks into the young eyes that, in her words, "hold wonder like a cup," and says, "You are a very, very bright child. You are going to succeed. You are going to produce. I will never let you fail. I promise you that!" As one of her former students recalled on *60 Minutes,* twenty years after he had been in Marva's classroom, "When somebody does that every day for two years, it transforms you!" That is the impact an inspirational mentor can have.

Mentors such as Marva Collins achieve titanic accomplishments because they inspire. And they inspire because they live the principles they teach. Every mentor must aspire to do the same.

Network

A good mentor introduces the protégé to other people who can also provide support, information, and resources. Networking is vital to effective functioning in the real world, and the mentor should give the protégé a head start on establishing those key contacts.

It takes years to cultivate and build a network of friends and associates of sufficient breadth and depth to be useful in a wide range of situations. One of the greatest resources an "old head" owns is a network of people who can help cut through the usual tangle of red tape and quickly obtain the desired result. These contacts are enormously valuable shortcuts who effectively reduce untold hours wasted in researching issues from scratch or running into bureaucratic roadblocks. In some cases, it is literally impossible to accomplish a given task without the extra boost a good network can supply. When something must get done, reliance on such a network is a tremendous force multiplier.

Of course, a mentor cannot simply deliver a network to a protégé as if it were a notebook. Relationships are nontransferable . . . at least not directly transferable. But it is possible to act as a go-between and a facilitator. The mentor should personally take the protégé to meet as many contacts as feasible, one at a time, in their respective work areas. These meetings should be rather informal, under pleasant, ice-breaking conditions, with an eye toward helping the protégé establish a relationship with each contact.

The very act of physically accompanying the protégé on a series of personal visits to meet and chat with contacts is a valuable lesson because it will demonstrate the importance of getting out from behind the desk, escaping from the office, and interacting with people face-to-face. Particularly in this electronic age of e-mail, voice mail, cell phones, and faxes, it is very easy to lose the personal touch that is so central to effective networking. No matter how high-tech our society becomes, human beings relate much more naturally to each other than to any other means of communication no matter how convenient or timely. Mentors must show how to use, cultivate, and keep a network flourishing, *now* more than ever.

The mentor should supplement a personal visit to each contract with a list of people, addresses, office locations, telephone numbers, and e-mail addresses, complete with a brief description of who they are and what they do. The network is too important to entrust it entirely to the protégé's memory; a written record will be a valuable insurance policy for the protégé to rely on. Plus, the list may serve to jog the mentor's memory of each contact and lead to further helpful insights.

In addition to sharing a personal preexisting network with the protégé, the mentor should teach the protégé how to build upon this nucleus and add contacts of his or her own. The art of being a professional friend, exchanging legitimate favors and serving as a prized contact for other people, is a vital lesson for the mentor to convey. This is the type of real-world practical skill that is an ideal subject for mentoring.

Goal-set

Many young and inexperienced people fail to understand the importance of setting proper goals and objectives or they lack the expertise to make their goals realistic and attainable. Mentors set goals, teach the need for goal-setting, and help their protégés master the process of establishing and effectively pursuing goals.

First, an integral part of the organizational aspect of mentoring is to set goals. Very early in the relationship with the protégé, the mentor should carefully establish some tangible goals to achieve with the protégé. As always, the goals should be worthwhile, specific, attainable, measurable, and have a timetable. This is critically important because the goals will be the target for everything that is done from that point on, the end toward which all efforts are directed. Once the goals are established, the mentor should periodically monitor progress toward attaining each goal (and milestones along the way) and make any necessary adjustments to the goals.

All of the mentors discussed in this chapter are outstanding examples of people who set highly challenging, worthy goals and then did everything necessary to achieve them. Jackie Robinson, Anne Sullivan, Jaime Escalante, Socrates, and Marva Collins knew exactly what they wanted to achieve, and they devoted themselves to their goals with magnificent persistence and dedication. Their single-minded pursuit of deeply felt goals–goals that motivated them from the very core of their hearts–enabled them to achieve vertiginous heights against incredible odds. Even our fictional example, Don Quixote, displayed legendary commitment to the vision that impelled him to his feats of courage and devotion. Despite of–or was it because of–his failure to see the flaws in his "impossible dream," he conquered obstacles that would have persuaded others to surrender. His story still has the power to stir our hearts hundreds of years after it was written because all of us hunger to have our lives count and to know that we have given our best in pursuit of a noble cause.

In addition to setting and stressing the importance of goals for the mentoring process, a mentor must also teach proper goal-setting techniques. Many young people confuse goals with wishes and fail to grasp the elements that are essential to transforming mere wishful thinking into an attainable and worthwhile plan for the future. Also, in today's culture of instant gratification and minuscule attention spans, some people have never learned the discipline that is so central to the determined pursuit of a clearly defined goal. It is not uncommon for people to be unfamiliar with the very concept of deferred gratification, let alone be able to implement it. A mentor's work is not done until the protégé moves beyond that level into the realm of a mature goal-setter and goal-achiever.

An excellent way of doing this is to meet privately with the protégé and let the person talk about background, goals (both near- and long-term), and hopes and dreams. The mentor can share present and past goals with the protégé, too, and in so doing illustrate by example some of the factors the mentor has used in his or her own goal setting.

This will highlight some of the elements the protégé may have omitted and vividly demonstrate how they contribute to making goals realistic in concept and reality in execution. It should become apparent to the protégé that there are significant differences between workable goals on the one hand and pleasant but less reality-based dreams, hopes, or wishes on the other.

The mentor should teach the principles of effective goal setting and guide the protégé to gradually develop and refine goals, objectives, milestones, measures of progress, and to a plan of action.

Conclusion

This chapter has examined the mentoring process within an analytical framework that identified the key elements of effective mentoring. Through the study and evaluation of these principles as practiced by several notable examples, you can gain a working understanding of what it takes to be a mentor. Ultimately, however, it is only through actually trying these principles that you will truly learn what they mean. The learning curve will probably be neither smooth nor easy. But "mentor" is not a title we can arrogate to ourselves or have bestowed upon us through a simple administrative act.

It is an honor that must be earned every day as we diligently strive to apply each of the principles.

If we succeed, it will be because we have learned how to use mentoring as a tool kit for our time machine. Through effective implementation of the tools that are the mentoring principles, we will influence the future and change the course of events in ways both great and small. As mentors, our greatest reward may be one day to witness our former protégés in turn become mentors.

A major challenge of contemporary organizations is to nurture the talent and interest of all employees so that the needs of education, government, military, business and other professional fields can be met. To achieve this worthy goal, leaders must take seriously their obligation to mentor their people, if they expect them to meet the needs of society in a world as complex as we live in today. Mentors must have the vision to develop the leadership potential in employees for the global and highly inter-dependent world of the future.

Discussion Questions and Ideas

- What is mentoring and why is it important? Who should be a mentor? How do we find a mentor? How and when do we mentor?

- Is mentoring a productivity multiplier? Why? What are some of the important factors to consider in mentoring?

- Can you be a mentor to anyone in your life right now? Do you need a mentor?

- Which of the people described in this chapter best exemplify the type of mentor you aspire to be?

- Why is mentoring a leadership obligation and responsibility?

- Does mentoring occur naturally or can it be cultivated? Why are mentor/protégé relationships actively encouraged in organizations today?

- Who have you known who was a great mentor? Why were they so successful?

- Can you add more examples of notable mentors to those listed under each of the elements of mentoring in this chapter?

- How can mentor/protégé relationships be made more meaningful and productive for both parties?

Bibliography and Recommended Readings

Barna, George. *Turning Visions into Action*. Ventura, California: Regal Books, 1996.

Bjornson, Richard, ed. "Approaches to Teaching Cervantes' Don Quixote." *Modern Language Association of America*, New York: 1984.

Collins, Marva. *Ordinary Children, Extraordinary Teachers*. Charlottesville, VA:1992.

Collins, Marva and Civia Tamarkin. *Marva Collins' Way*. New York: J. P. Tarcher, 1990.

Covey, Stephen R. *The 7 Habits of Highly Successful People*. New York: Simon & Schuster, 1992.

Cervantes, Minguel de. *Adventures of Don Quixote*. New York: Penguin, 1988.

Engelmann, Siegfried; Phyllis Haddox; and *Elaine* Bruner. *Teach Your Child to Read in One Hundred Easy Lessons*. New York: Simon & Schuster, 1983.

Fortgang, Laura Berman. *Take Yourself to the Top: The Secrets of America's # 1 Career Coach*. New York: Warner Books, 1998.

Geiger-Dumond, Adrianne and Susan Boyle. "Mentoring: A Practitioner's Guide." *Training and Development*, March 1995.

Gibson, William. *Miracle Worker*. New York: Bantam Books, 1984.

Huang, A. and Lynch J. *Mentoring*. New York: Harper-Collins, 1995.

Kleinman, Carol. *The Career Coach*. Chicago: Dearborn-Financial Publishing, 1994.

McClenahen, John. "One-on-One Career Coaches." *Government Executive*, July 1990.

Murray, Margo. *Beyond the Myths and Magic of Mentoring: How to Facilitate an Effective Mentoring Program*. San Francisco: Jossey-Bass, 1991.

Rampersad, Arnold and Jackie Rampersad. *Jackie Robinson: A Biography*. New York: Knopf, 1997.

Robinson, Jackie and Alford Duckett. *I Never Had It Made: An Autobiography*. New York: Ecco Press, 1995.

Salisbury, Frank. *Developing Managers as Coaches: A Trainer's Guide*. New York: McGraw-Hill, 1994.

Shea, Gordon. *Mentoring*. New York: American Management Association, 1994.

Smith, Justin. *Mentoring in the Air Force*. Maxwell Air Force, Alabama, 1996.

Stevens, Paul. *How to Network and Select a Mentor*. England: Resource Publications, Inc., 1995.

Tygiel, Jules. *Baseball's Great Experiment: Jackie Robinson and His Legacy*. London: Oxford University Press, 1997.

"You Can't Float to the Top." *Government Executive*. June, 1998.

Chapter 5

Leadership and the Art of Feedback

Executive Summary

One of the key proficiencies a good leader must possess is the art of giving and receiving feedback. All of the other tools of leadership combined will not allow anyone to be fully effective if feedback is lacking. The vision, talents, and competencies of both the leader and the followers will not interconnect in true synergy without this vital link, this bridge, this lifeline.

It is through feedback that we put into practice the ability to see ourselves as others see us. Conversely, it is through feedback that others know how we see and perceive them. Feedback is any kind of return information or instruction from a source which is helpful in regulating behavior. It takes the form of verbal or nonverbal communication to a person or group, providing them with information about how their behavior is perceived by one or more individuals, especially as it relates to a goal or standard. Feedback can also be defined as a reaction by others to how one's behavior is affecting them, usually in terms of their emotions and perceptions. This chapter proposes that free, open, and honest feedback is most effective when delivered in a productive and positive attempt to improve performance. Without constructive feedback, the performer has no way of knowing if his or her performance is adequate or what has to be done to improve it. It is important when giving feedback to let a person know where he or she stands in relation to an established goal or standard of acceptable behavior.

The authors address the subject of feedback from an analytical, descriptive, and prescriptive approach. This is accomplished by recounting how feedback works, especially as a source of information and as a root of motivation, both of which are intended to improve performance. The analytical framework set forth in this chapter addresses the term "feedback" as an acronym, each letter of which stands for one of its important component parts. This approach is designed to serve as a mnemonic device to remind leaders how to conduct effective feedback. The essential quality and spirit of feedback is to comfort the afflicted and to afflict the comfortable. Giving and receiving feedback is seldom easy, but it is necessary for effective leadership to take place, and it is an art that can be learned, practiced, and constantly improved.

Discussion

Effective feedback for some people is an unnatural act; however, it can still become second nature to everyone, even if it is not part of our "first nature." This process of making feedback part of our repertoire of leadership skills requires two simple, but perhaps unfamiliar, things: We have to develop an understanding of what feedback really is and then recognize when we are giving feedback and when we are not.

This chapter provides a model for understanding feedback and suggests a strategy for implementing it.

Anyone who has ever been an employee has experienced the power a supervisor has to make life miserable for subordinates. Conversely, anyone who has ever been higher up the organizational chart knows that a supervisor's success or failure is, to a very great extent, dependent on the competence, diligence, and motivation of the workers. Ideally, and out of sheer self-interest, this reciprocal arrangement generates a symbiosis wherein supervisors and subordinates strive to satisfy the wishes and needs of each other and their customers. But, in reality, the workplace often closely resembles a dysfunctional family more akin to the Simpsons than the Waltons. Although pain is an integral part of organizational life, misery is an option. Feedback as presented in this chapter is intended to ease some of the pain often associated with performance feedback.

Why do so many bosses and employees seem to be in disparate, polarized realms, superficially belonging to the same organization yet pulling in opposite directions? If, indeed, it is in the self-interest of both leadership and the employees to share useful information and interact with respect and openness, what causes the model to break down? The answer lies hidden beneath the debris that human beings typically generate as they struggle to coexist with fellow members of the species *Homo sapiens*. Underneath all the inefficiency, conflict, confusion, resentment, and misunderstanding lurk both the culprit and the solution: feedback. The importance of feedback is no secret to the leaders who have been doing the job "in the trenches." For example, please refer to Figure 1. This identifies the top ten leadership and management concerns as perceived by 508 personnel in twelve diverse work groups in the United States Air Force. Lack of feedback on performance is ranked third in this group of ten concerns. Figure 2 is a cumulative, rank-order listing of the survey participants.

Feedback can be understood as feeding the hands that back us. Both supervisors and subordinates must be *backed* or supported by each other if they are to succeed either individually or collectively as a key component of a thriving and surviving organization. But in order to receive this backing, and have it be as effective as possible, both supervisors and subordinates must feed each other the information necessary to do the work and keep the people productive and content. Everyone in an organization is realistically in the *hands* of the other members of that organization; each person's potential is firmly related to the attitude and aptitude of all the people around them. When feedback is given infrequently or inadequately and is thus counterproductive, it can cripple individuals and the component organization. Only through feeding the hands that back us can we achieve the symbiosis necessary for mutual success.

This point can be illustrated with a story. A young person goes to study with a great teacher and asks: "I would like to know the difference between heaven and hell." The teacher says, "That's very easy. Hell is a place where there is a great banquet with great and wonderful things to eat. The problem is that everyone is starving to death because in order to get the food to their mouth, they have to eat with a four-foot fork and they cannot seem to do it. Conversely, heaven is a place where there is a great banquet with many great things to eat, but everyone is eating. They, too, have to eat with four-foot forks. The only difference is the people in heaven are feeding each other." Feedback helps us feed one another and provide the nourishment to better sustain organizational life. While the positive effect of feedback on performance is one of the most accepted principles in organizational psychology, it is also one of the most difficult tasks facing supervisors.

Providing constructive and evaluative feedback needed to help subordinates develop professionally is clearly a major leadership responsibility. Conducting feedback successfully requires honesty, skill, courage, and respect, not only for one-self but for the person to whom feedback is being given. The term *feedback* as used herein is derived from the field of cy-bernetics in that it relates to a system based on source infor-mation to change behavior. Its basic assumption is that feed-back should be helpful to the person or persons receiving it.

In this chapter we will focus on feedback from a super-visor to a subordinate; however, the principles discussed are equally applicable to feedback from subordinate to supervi-sor. In a fully functional organization, both are essential. In fact, feedback must include a two-way flow of information if it is to be effective; in this sense, it is impossible to isolate supervisor-to-subordinate feedback from its complement, subordinate-to-supervisor feedback. The two are interrelated and intertwined, and ideally should always be found in tan-dem, as the wheels of a bicycle.

"TOP TEN LEADERSHIP AND MANAGEMENT CONCERNS" (TTLMC)

A = 508 1 = Lowest Concern 10 = Highest Concern	M-M	DP	LG GP CC	NCO	CPO	CAP CH	CAP WG CC	ANGF	ANGP	OPS SQ CC	WAG	SOS
INEFFECTIVE COMMUNICATION	10	8	10	10	9	10	10	10	10	10	2	10
EXCESS OF CRISIS MANAGEMENT	9	10	9	7	7	9	8	8	7	9	9	3
LACK OF FEEDBACK ON PERFORMANCE	3	5	8	9	6	6	9	7	8	4	8	9
NO OR INAPPROPRIATE GOAL SETTING	8	6	4	6	3	8	6	5	6	5	7	7
NOT ENOUGH TRAINING	5	3	5	8	4	7	7	4	4	6	10	6
LACK OF OPPORTUNITY FOR ADVANCEMENT	6	2	6	4	10	4	3	9	9	8	3	5
REWARDS NOT RELATED TO PERFORMANCE	4	9	3	3	5	5	5	6	2	3	5	8
UNREASONABLE WORKLOADS	2	4	7	1	8	3	4	3	3	2	4	4
BOSS WILL NOT LET ME DO MY JOB	7	7	2	2	2	1	1	1	1	7	6	2
LACK OF CHALLENGING WORK	1	1	1	5	1	2	2	2	5	1	1	1

FIGURE 1

"TOP TEN LEADERSHIP AND MANAGEMENT CONCERNS"
IDENTIFIES BY GROUP THE FOLLOWING AIR FORCE POPULATION

(508 Members) IN THIS SURVEY RESEARCH

M-M = Air Force personnel on site at Martin Marietta, Denver,
   Colorado (now Lockheed Martin Corporation)
DP = Directors of Personnel
LG GP CC = Logistics Group Commanders
NCO = Noncommissioned Officers
CPO = Civilian Personnel Officers
CAP CH = Civil Air Patrol – USAF, Chaplains
CAP WG CC = Civil Air Patrol – USAF, Wing Commanders
ANGF = Air National Guard Full Time
ANGP = Air National Guard Part Time
OPS SQ CC = Operations Squadron Commanders
WAG = Washington State Air National Guard, Command
   Leadership Academy
SOS = Squadron Officer School

"TOP TEN LEADERSHIP AND MANAGEMENT CONCERNS"
CUMULATIVE: 508 SURVEY PARTICIPANTS

INEFFECTIVE COMMUNICATIONS 9.0
EXCESS OF CRISIS MANAGEMENT 8.0
LACK OF FEEDBACK ON PERFORMANCE 7.0
NO OR INAPPROPRIATE GOAL SETTING 6.2
NOT ENOUGH TRAINING 5.7
LACK OF OPPORTUNITY FOR ADVANCEMENT 5.6
REWARDS NOT RELATED TO PERFORMANCE 4.9
UNREASONABLE WORKLOADS 3.9
BOSS WILL NOT LET ME DO MY JOB 3.2
LACK OF CHALLENGING WORK 1.8

FIGURE 2

*The variables in Figure 1 and Figure 2 replicate similar data first
identified by Working Woman magazine.*

Types of Feedback in the Workplace

The twin purposes of feedback from a supervisor to an employee are to inform and to motivate the employee. If either purpose is not achieved, the employee's performance will suffer. And due to the interrelatedness of the performance or success of all members of an organization, the supervisor will suffer as well; thus, all concerned own the problem.

Informational feedback may take various forms, depending on the length of time an employee has been in the organization, organizational changes, and quality of the employee's work. With informational feedback, the assumption is that subordinates want to do a good job. Therefore, telling them the results of their performance has a high probability of leading to improved future achievement. Some examples of informational feedback include:

- Clarification of the employee's areas of responsibility and specific duties within each area of responsibility

- Discussion of the performance standards the employee is expected to meet

- Specifics of employee's prior performance, including areas for improvement

The most crucial time for informational feedback is the period immediately following the arrival of either the employee or the supervisor in the organization. At this early relationship stage, inertia and routinization are at their lowest ebb and opportunities for meaningful change are at their zenith. Clear, detailed, and effective feedback then can obviate the need for corrective actions later.

Motivational feedback would also be important in such a working environment but as with its informational cousin, is best used consistently from the beginning rather than as part of crisis management. Motivational feedback is designed to inspire, to inculcate values, to activate, and to encourage people.

The following are some examples of motivational feedback:

- Praise and recognition for a job well done

- Praise for a positive attitude

- Explanation of how a good performance could be made even better

- Discussion of significance of employee's work as related to the organizational mission

- Explanation of the importance of the organizational mission

- Encouragement and offers of help in overcoming employee areas of difficulty

- Discussion of the benefits the employee would derive from excellent performance

- Discussion of the negative consequences to the employee resulting from poor performance

All of these with the exception of the last are positive "carrots" rather than negative or threatening "sticks." Each person uniquely responds to such things in an individual way, but most people are more effectively motivated on a long-term basis by a pat on the back than a kick in the pants.

As with any type of feedback, timing is important to its impact. It would, therefore, be advisable to include some or all of these positive varieties of motivational feedback in an early one-on-one session whenever there is a new employee-supervisor relationship. This would help create an upbeat tone for the worker at the very beginning.

To provide a framework within which we can analyze the ingredients of effective feedback–whether informational or motivational or a hybrid of the two–we will now examine feedback as an acronym. By considering the attributes of effective feedback in this way, the word "feedback" itself may prove to be a mnemonic device enabling leaders to recall these key points in real-world settings.

Ingredients of Effective Feedback

Feedback may be viewed as an acronym, consisting of the adjectives that describe an effective and positive leadership approach:

> **F**requent
> **E**arly
> **E**vidence-based
> **D**ialogue-oriented
> **B**eneficial
> **A**ccurate
> **C**lear
> **K**ind

We will consider each of these elements in turn.

Frequent

When feedback mechanisms become institutionalized and routine, they fall prey to the same bureaucratic maladies that afflict everything a large organization attempts to mandate. If worker appraisal or rating feedback is required on an annual or semiannual basis, then that is generally how often managers will give feedback–irrespective of their workers' requirements.

Feedback need not be squeezed into the narrow confines of formal, official "report cards." Feedback is–or should be–a response to a need. It is senseless to postpone satisfying that need until some artificially imposed day shows up on the calendar. Leaders must always remain alert to the need or an opportunity for giving feedback. When such occasions arise, they should give feedback as soon as possible.

By giving feedback frequently, managers ensure that their people are receiving regular "preventive maintenance." Whether the workers are doing particularly well or particularly poorly, or, conversely, are excelling in some areas and needing improvement in others, frequent feedback serves as an automatic pilot. It serves to keep the workers on the same course, when they are heading in the right direction, and it can be a mid-course correction when they are deviating from the desired heading. Only by frequently making these minor adjustments can leaders always keep their employees on track. If they delay until the next "official" feedback session is due, the situation may be much worse if not out of control.

Some supervisors may be under the impression that all feedback sessions must be formal, official, full-fledged occasions for a thorough evaluation of the employee's entire work performance. While such macro-feedback sessions are important, much more narrowly tailored and informal micro-feedback sessions are also vital to successful day-to-day operations in the workplace. Not every session need be lengthy and all-encompassing. Whenever a problem (or an achievement) arises, that is an opportunity for effective feedback. Frequent feedback enables leaders to accentuate the positive and eliminate the negative from their workers' repertoire of behaviors. The most immediate and opportune moment is the most effective time.

Finally, another advantage of frequent feedback sessions is that they obviate the need to address numerous points at any one time. As with any information-sharing situation, whether it be in a classroom setting or a workplace, people can only absorb a finite amount of material in a given session. If all discussion topics are hoarded for one protracted annual or semiannual binge, the employee will probably be overwhelmed by the sheer quantity of material and will eventually go numb and tune out any further input. But by giving frequent feedback, leaders can cover fewer issues and thereby improve the odds that the employee will learn something beneficial from the experience.

Early

The earlier feedback begins in the employee-employer relationship, the better the chances are for a successful partnership. And generally the earlier feedback is given following an example of desirable or undesirable behavior the more likely the feedback will succeed either in reinforcing or discouraging such behavior.

The initial interactions between any two people are important in setting the tone for the relationship. Human beings tend to form persistent opinions concerning each other at a very early stage, so it is crucial the proper foundation be laid for future cooperation. As soon as possible after meeting an employee, a supervisor should have at least an informal feedback session to discuss personal backgrounds, the mission of the organization, the nature and scope of the employee's duties, and the significance of those duties to the attainment of organizational and personal goals. If this first feedback session is a positive experience for the employee, it will be far easier to maintain effective feedback throughout the working relationship. The worker will know what is expected and why it is important to perform well and will feel like a valued part of a worthwhile enterprise. Subsequent feedback will find a receptive listener when the supervisor builds on the initial foundation to provide effective guidance early and often.

It is axiomatic that reinforcement, both positive and negative, is most likely to work when it immediately follows the conduct in question. When feedback comes early, the conduct is still fresh in the mind of the person who did it, and the lesson will have its highest probability of being remembered. But when weeks or months separate the behavior from the feedback, it is much more difficult to recall exactly what was done and why it was done. The feedback will, therefore, be less effective.

The ideal time to give feedback is very soon after the behavior takes place. A quick, early response has the best chance of ensuring that desirable actions continue and undesirable actions stop. This is a corollary to the principle that feedback should be frequent; by not waiting until official evaluation time to provide input, a leader can influence his or her people with maximum efficacy.

Evidence-based

When feedback is intended to be corrective or to adjust a worker's behavior to make it more acceptable, it is crucial that the feedback be based on clear evidence. The employee should be shown proof of what happened and why it ought to be improved. There is nothing more effective than providing a good example.

This does not mean a supervisor should confront a subordinate with a mountain of evidence and use it as the basis for a searing cross-examination. Such an approach would be certain to put the employee instantly on the defensive. Instead, the supervisor should use specific, verifiable examples of work or other behavior to illustrate the points being made.

Feedback is essentially a method of teaching. Teachers are more successful in helping their students learn when their lessons are fortified with actual examples from the students' own experiences. These examples enable the students to place the lesson in a meaningful context, in a reality-based frame of reference. Specific examples also allow students to personally see that the lesson is true because they can verify its validity from firsthand knowledge and experience.

An employee who receives feedback without any evidence or examples of the behavior in question has no foundation for improvement. He or she may doubt the truthfulness of the unsupported assertions and so dismiss any suggestions for change. But when supervisors include evidence in their feedback sessions, it becomes both a teaching experience and a learning outcome.

Even where the feedback is positive, if it lacks solid evidence, its useful effect will be greatly diminished. If an employee is praised only with nebulous generalities, such as "you are doing a great job," he or she will have no way of knowing exactly what warranted the recognition and will be unsure which behaviors need to continue or cease. Similarly, if the employee feels the praise is undeserved or unwarranted, he or she may resent it and feel patronized. Specific examples of the good work, and evidence of why it is important, will avoid both the appearance and the actuality of a patronizing attitude on the supervisor's part.

One significant component of evidence-based feedback is a written record of the feedback session itself. This can be as formal or informal as is warranted under the circumstances, but at a minimum there should be a brief summary of topics discussed and a synopsis of the employee's response. This memorandum can be partially prepared in advance to serve as an organizational framework and agenda for the session. It should be dated and signed or initialed by both parties at the conclusion of the session if possible. Thereafter, the feedback memorandum can be kept on file and used as a positive leadership tool. It may be useful as a memory jogger for the supervisor and as documentation of prior attempts to correct a given problem should the situation deteriorate or fail to improve.

Dialogue-oriented

Feedback is least effective when it is a one-way street. When the supervisor uses the session as a forum to deliver a monologue or to hand out a previously written document, information is flowing only in one direction. Feedback, however, requires a two-way flow.

One of the purposes of a feedback session is for the supervisor to learn what the subordinate thinks and feels. The leader may be unaware of factors that are affecting the worker's productivity or attitude. If so, the best way to learn about them is from the person who knows best. A key element of feedback is a positive regard for others, that is, bringing out the best in other people.

If the supervisor uses the entire feedback session solely as an opportunity to pontificate, the employee will learn nothing from the experience. Moreover, this person will probably feel mistreated and manipulated, handled more like an inanimate tool than a human being. The process will be more productive for everyone if there is a dialogue between supervisor and subordinate. Only in this way can information pass in both directions and only in this way can both people learn something. It is indeed a rare occasion if one learns anything by simply talking. It is probably for this reason that we have two ears and one mouth, the intention being that we should listen at least twice as much as we talk.

A vital component of dialogue is that both parties listen empathically to what the other is saying. A leader may be prepared to enter a feedback session primed to deliver a speech on how the employee needs to improve; but there must also be room left for the leader to quiet down and absorb what the employee has to say as well. Likewise, it is impossible to listen effectively while talking or thinking about the next point one wants to make. If the supervisor expects the employee to listen to him or her, then the supervisor should reciprocate with the same courtesy. And by listening the supervisor just might learn something.

We all engage in dialogue-oriented feedback many times, every day, in our ordinary conversations with friends and acquaintances. In these chats, we naturally exchange information on a mutual basis, not just in one direction.

We give each other eye contact, respond with verbal and non-verbal acknowledgment to each other's comments, and genuinely pay full attention by listening to what is said. We are reasonably polite and try not to interrupt; everyone gets a chance to talk. There is no reason to check our common sense at the door when we go to a feedback session. We can and should use all of these standard communication techniques during our feedback sessions; they are normal and natural because they work and have worked for millennia. They will work in feedback sessions in the workplace just as they have worked in billions of conversations and casual exchanges since humans learned how to talk.

As Stephen R. Covey points out in his *Seven Habits of Highly Effective People,* empathic communication means seeking first to understand and then to be understood. This requires us to concentrate on the content, emotion, body language, and underlying feelings of the other person's communication. Rather than paying only partial attention so that we can think about our response, we must focus fully on the other person and try to understand what he or she is expressing. See through his or her eyes and feel with his or her heart before switching gears to the response mode. One little-used but extremely helpful technique in this regard is for the supervisor to turn the tables and periodically to allow the employees to rate him or her. The supervisor can develop a standard form which divides into as many specific categories as seems necessary to obtain usable information. One example is Figure 3. The employees are allowed to turn in their forms anonymously if they wish, to remove any fear or hesitancy they might otherwise feel in rating their boss. The experience can be enormously empowering and enlightening for the employees as they become aware that their opinions matter and that their boss needs feedback every bit as much as they do. Equally important, the supervisor can learn, from those who know best, exactly what he or she needs to do to become a more effective leader. Regular use of "boss evaluations" is a very powerful application of dialogue-oriented feedback that can pay huge dividends in terms of employee morale and organizational effectiveness.

Beneficial

It should be obvious that any feedback should be beneficial to the person receiving it; otherwise, it serves no constructive purpose. But every supervisor must keep this overarching goal in mind at all times in the feedback process; the goal is to improve the employee and to enhance mission accomplishment. Everything must be examined and evaluated to ensure that it will further rather than obstruct the intended purpose of effective feedback.

In this regard, the supervisor should strive to give a positive tone to the feedback session. If criticisms are needed, it is best to put them in the context of the more favorable aspects of the employee's work. If a spoonful of sugar helps the medicine go down, then including some worker achievements and value to the organization will make them more receptive to improvement suggestions. Otherwise, the feedback may actually prove counterproductive, be discouraging to the employee, and generate feelings of hopelessness and failure.

It is not enough to fix the blame; we must also help to fix the problem. The supervisor should never simply point out the employee's failings and leave it at that. The feedback session is not complete until the employee is also offered, or preferably helped to arrive at, one or more possible solutions. The deed should be the primary subject of feedback–not the doer.

One of the most beneficial aspects of feedback is, in fact, a participative dialogue in which supervisor and employee work together to brainstorm ways of dealing with any existing difficulties that may exist. Such a synergistic, interdependent, cooperative approach recognizes the partnership relationship between the parties and allows both to grow and learn through the problem-solving process. This process is far more beneficial to the employee and to the long-term future of the organization than the quicker but passive spoon-feeding approach wherein the supervisor merely tells the employee what to do as well as when, where, and how to do it.

Evaluation of the Boss

INSTRUCTIONS TO THE EVALUATOR: Completion of this form is voluntary–you do not have to evaluate me if you do not want to. Your signature at the end is also *optional.* The purpose of this evaluation is to help me, as the boss, improve my management and leadership skills by identifying strengths as well as areas where improvement is needed.

Do not let personal feelings affect your rating–rate only on performance, not on personality. Base your evaluation on my typical performance for the entire period, not on isolated incidents which are not typical. You should be able to support your ratings with comments and examples that are as specific and factual as possible, to help me improve.

When you are finished, please place the completed form in my in-box. You may type the form if you wish it to be totally anonymous. *Thank you* for your time! I truly appreciate your honest, candid feedback.

	Outstanding	Excellent	Good	Fair	Poor
Sets a good example for others					
Creates a positive work environment					
Gives clear directions					
Is a good listener............................					
Plans and organizes well					
Is generally fair in decisions					
Gives regular feedback on performance					
Provides adequate support to do tasks					
Is willing to consider new ideas/suggestions...					
Is empathetic to workers' concerns					
Behaves in a professional manner					

Areas of Greatest Strength:

Areas Where Improvement Is Most Needed:

Other Comments:

_____   _____
Evaluator's Signature (totally optional)   Date

FIGURE 3

Accurate

Just as it is important that feedback be based on sound evidence, it is vital that feedback accurately reflect and logically flow from that evidence. Feedback that is inaccurate, whether because it is unfairly negative or unrealistically positive, is based on a faulty premise and is doomed to ineffectiveness in shaping the worker's behavior.

This is a particularly serious problem in some large organizations where formalized written evaluations are used. There is a strong tendency to inflate employee ratings, both numerical and narrative, for a variety of reasons. In part, rating inflation is a self-fulfilling phenomenon, fueled by the artificially high ratings other supervisors are giving to their people and the desire of each rater not to harm his or her subordinates by breaking from the pack and issuing accurate ratings. It is also psychologically easier on both rater and ratee when each evaluation is filled with fluffy "happy news" rather than hard, realistic facts. Good ratings are a conflict-avoidance device that helps keep peace in the workplace. Also, most supervisors enjoy feeling like "good guys" who help the people under their care by boosting careers and building them up with positive evaluations. It is much less stressful and more pleasant than directly confronting shortcomings. In other words, one way to keep people from jumping down your throat is to keep your mouth shut.

The difficulties with rating inflation are that it is dishonest, inaccurate, and a roadblock to effective feedback. When almost everyone receives top ratings, it becomes a formidable challenge to differentiate among employees on the basis of merit—they all look terrific! Sometimes an arcane system creeps in, where subtle shadings of word choice can reveal the true meaning of the evaluation, but only to the select few who know the code. To the average person, there would be no significant difference from one appraisal to another.

Inflated, inaccurate ratings force such "work-arounds" to enable leaders to properly make important personnel decisions despite the flood of top evaluations where almost all employees seem equally outstanding. But a harmful side-effect of this is the false impression left on the employees.

If a subordinate is continually given written appraisals filled with maximum ratings and "rave reviews," it is only natural for that person to believe that "all is well in River City." If all of an employee's evaluations proclaim only excellence, where is there room for improvement? The feedback value of inflated ratings is worse than zero–such inaccurate "information" is actually a detriment to both the employee and the organization. Even if a subordinate is aware of the endemic rating inflation, the natural human tendency is to believe one's own outstanding evaluations are entirely deserved and everyone else's are puffed up. As a result, all ratees will feel they are doing just fine. Any other feedback to the contrary can be dismissed as inconsistent with the formal, official evaluations. It can be exceedingly difficult to persuade an employee of the need for attitude or behavior adjustments in light of such formidable but misdirected official feedback.

No one wants to be the only person issuing accurate appraisals in an environment of widespread rating inflation. It would be unfair to the employees and would cause intense resentment toward the rater. What, then, can be done?

It is important to supplement any inflated official appraisals with genuine, informal feedback on a regular basis. At or near the time when the official ratings are issued, a private one-on-one meeting with the employee would afford an excellent opportunity to discuss the appraisal and inject some reality into the process. Such a contemporaneous meeting should ameliorate or prevent the problem of ratees believing their own glowing reviews. Much of the employee's work, in fact, may have been excellent, and there is no need to de-emphasize this. But where there is room for obvious improvement the supervisor should point this out as well, especially if such criticism, however slight, is as a practical matter banned from inclusion in official appraisals.

When combined with frequent informal feedback sessions at other times, this approach can guarantee each employee receives accurate information on which future actions can be based. Regular, frequent "reality checks" throughout the employment relationship, particularly where the supervisor ensures the feedback is meticulously evidence-based, should help exert some degree of gravitational pull on an employee who otherwise may tend to fly into orbit on the high-octane fuel of supercharged ratings. The sheer number and frequency of such doses of reality therapy can provide an effective antidote to the human instinct to believe our own halo-crowned appraisals.

Clear

A corollary of the accuracy principle is that feedback must be clear and should be communicated as such. If the message is garbled or sugar-coated, the employee may be unable to decipher the message and thus derive no benefit. Even worse the message may be misunderstood and misinterpreted and cause consequences very different from those the supervisor intended.

Winning can probably be best defined as the science of being totally prepared. Thus, it is counterproductive, both for supervisor and employee, to conduct a feedback session without careful preparation. The supervisor must go into the session with a concrete, specific purpose, with focus on that purpose. This will involve pulling together any relevant documents, gathering information from other managers, and developing a concrete plan for the feedback session. A short agenda or a simple outline will help the supervisor stay organized and on track and can serve as a reminder of the key points to be made and evidence or examples to be discussed.

During the preparatory phase, the supervisor should decide how he or she can best phrase key elements of the feedback, especially where a sensitive or emotional issue is involved. The meaning and the impact of the feedback can be diminished if the supervisor hems and haws, struggles for the right words, and appears unsure and disorganized during the feedback session. The risk of misunderstanding and confusion will be eased by a few carefully selected words, chosen in the less stressful atmosphere that prevails before the session begins. In giving good feedback, leaders ask two key questions: What is its purpose? What strategy will accomplish that purpose?

It is helpful to use this simple formula in addressing problems clearly:

- Diagnosis - a concise headline-type statement of the problem

- Example - one or more specific instances in which the problem arose, complete with evidentiary support

- Rationale - an explanation of why the behavior in question is undesirable, including the effect on the organization's mission or on other workers

- Prescription - a discussion, with employee input, of how the situation can be rectified

By following this method, the supervisor ensures each problem area is thoroughly and logically addressed and includes an action plan for resolution.

The second main pitfall in the area of clarity is the temptation to sugar-coat feedback. As with the tendency toward rating inflation, many supervisors attempt to soften the blow of criticism by applying liberal amounts of cosmetics. Uncomfortable with direct, plain-spoken, constructive criticism, they decorate the unpleasant realities with qualifiers," wigglewording" their way out of the "bad guy" role. Unfortunately, too many "sort of/kind of" qualifiers dilute the message and lessen its import to the recipient. After all, if the supervisor is unsure the employee needs to improve, why should the employee do anything about it?

While it is important to be sensitive to the employee's feelings, it is equally essential that the message not be sacrificed in the bargain. Ultimately, the focal point of the feedback must be brought into the open, with clarity, or else the entire exercise may be futile.

The only way a leader can be certain the message has been clearly expressed is to ask for and receive feedback from the recipient. By engaging the employee in a dialogue and asking for restatement or rephrasing of the key points, the supervisor can conduct an instant quality control check on the clarity and efficacy of the message. This discussion of main topics will allow the supervisor to detect and correct any misunderstandings or gaps in the employee's interpretation of the supervisor's meaning. Only when the employee is able to put the supervisor's comments in the employee's own words and discuss them with some insight can the supervisor be confident the message passed from one mind to the other without hopeless distortion.

Kind

Some supervisors have an austere, no-nonsense approach to their job and may come across as mean-spirited bullies. An authoritarian leadership style can include a "wall-to-wall" method of providing feedback, in which the employee feels attacked, threatened, insulted, and abused—or, in short, laid out and nailed down like wall-to-wall carpeting.

Aside from any moral or religious edicts to treat others as we would like to be treated, there are excellent functional/ utilitarian reasons to be kind to employees during feedback sessions. When people perceive themselves as mistreated or under siege, they naturally become defensive. Once those invisible shields are raised around a person's psyche, little, if any, information can penetrate. The supervisor might as well stop talking at that point because no additional message will override the "ATTACK" signals that have already been received, loud and clear.

It is imperative that feedback be limited to things that are within the power of the recipient to alter. It would be unkind in the extreme to criticize persons for something beyond their control. Everyone has limitations, whether physical, mental, or emotional. Feedback must take these limitations into account or else it will offend and alienate the person to whom it is directed. Similarly, if a given task is not properly within an employee's area of responsibility, it would be unfair and unkind to fault him or her for failing to perform it until and unless the employee is told about the new duties.

The need to provide feedback in a kind, nonthreatening way sometimes leads to the sugar-coating tendency that robs the message of its clarity, as discussed in the previous section. However, there need not be any conflict between the principles of clarity and kindness. A supervisor can communicate plainly and clearly, in an organized, focused manner, yet still be constructive, helpful, and considerate of the employee's feelings.

It is ultimately in the employee's best interests to be informed of any deficiencies identified by the supervisor. If a worker is not performing acceptably, there will eventually be negative consequences to that worker's career . . . unless someone notices the problem and corrects it. This is the concept of constructive criticism; it does people no favors to conceal or soft-pedal information that would help them to rectify something they are doing wrong. One can be kind without being weak or wishy-washy. So long as the supervisor makes it clear that he or she appreciates the subordinate's efforts and is offering some recommendations for improvement that would benefit everyone involved, the supervisor should feel free to set forth all relevant facts without apology or equivocation.

The ingredients of effective feedback as shown in this acronym emphasize that feedback is not only the breakfast of organizational champions, it is lunch and dinner, too. As Ken Blanchard has said, "Feedback properly conducted nudges people in the right direction. Feedback is a gift we give to others." The effective application of this simple feedback formula is a key tool used by many successful leaders–it just might work for you. It establishes the foundation for leaders to maintain an open and responsible dialogue with people. And in so doing, feedback serves as a catalyst to lower the ineffective communication barrier as shown in Figure 1. Handling feedback in this way can have a positive effect on unit cohesion, effectiveness, and productivity.

A key characteristic of leadership is that leaders simply give more. If people have the appropriate ambition, values, and expertise, they have the potential to lead. However, these characteristics must be coupled with the quality of giving more in the face of continuing challenges. Individuals who are concerned with only getting more will not make the grade. Unfortunately, most of us are more concerned with getting than giving. Perhaps this is one significant reason why genuine leadership is so rarely evident. Feedback as presented in this chapter is a form of giving. Good leaders understand that feedback is truly a gift they give others. In sum, the power of feedback opens the door to maximizing the effectiveness of our most valuable resource–our people.

Conclusion

The cliché talks about biting the hand that feeds us. In employment situations, each of us is fed in a literal as well as a figurative sense by the people above and below us in the organizational hierarchy. If we fail to give feedback, or are ineffective in the feedback methods we use, we are biting the hands that feed us and ultimately are harming ourselves as well as the people we supervise.

This chapter is meant to help every leader and manager achieve the opposite result. By providing our employees with information, giving proper attention to all of the attributes of effective feedback, we are feeding the hands that back us. In so doing, we benefit our workers, our organization, and ourselves. We increase the chances that each of us will be a survivor.

Discussion Questions and Ideas

- What is feedback? Why should feedback be given? Do you consider feedback to be a leadership responsibility? Why?

- What types of feedback have you encountered in the workplace? Was the feedback you received effective? Why or why not?

- What should be fed back in feedback? What should be the source of information used in providing feedback? How should feedback be delivered?

- Your boss does not give you any feedback. You want some; what do you do, and how do you do it?

- In giving feedback, can you be totally honest and totally considerate at the same time?

- How important is feedback to you?

- How is the practice of attentive listening related to feedback?

- What problems have you encountered in giving feedback? What have you done to solve these problems? What have you learned from the experience?

- How does one know when a feedback session is due?

- Have you ever been in a situation where periodic feedback was routinized and mandatory and became virtually meaningless, a ritualistic exercise in form over substance? If so, why did this happen? What could have prevented it?

- Is feedback given in your organization? If so, what is the quality of this feedback? Can it be improved; if so, how?

- Who must give and receive feedback?

Bibliography and Recommended Readings

Benjamin, A. *The Helping Interview.* Boston: Houghton Mifflin Co, 1987.

Blanchard, K. and S. Johnson. *The One Minute Manager.* La Jolla, CA: Blanchard-Johnson Publishers, 1981.

Chaplin, J. *The Dictionary of Psychology.* New York: Dell Publishing Co, 1968.

Chapman, E. *Leadership.* New York: Macmillan, 1989.

Connellan, T. "Interpersonal Feedback." *Quality Progress*, Milwaukee, WI, June 1991.

Covey, S. *Seven Habits of Highly Effective People*. New York: Fireside, 1989.

Department of the Air Force. Washington, D.C., Air Force Pamphlet 36-6, *USAF Officer's Guide*, 1988.

DePree, M. *Leadership Is An Art*. New York: Doubleday, 1989.

Ferris, G. and K. Rowland. *Performance Evaluation, Goal Setting, and Feedback*. Greenwich, CT: JAI Press, 1990.

Grove, A. *One-on-One with Andy Grove*. New York: Putnam, 1987.

Haynes, M. *Stepping Up to Supervisor*. Los Altos, CA: Crisp Publications Inc., 1990.

Hersey, P., and K. Blanchard. *Management of Organizational Behavior: Utilizing Human Resources*. Englewood Cliffs, NY: Prentice Hall, 1993.

"Issues and Observations." Center for Creative Leadership, Greensboro. NC (Winter, 1990).

Karrass, C. *The Negotiating Game*. New York: Crowell, 1970.

Kaufman,H. *Administrative Feedback*. Washington, D.C.: The Brookings Institution, 1973.

Maurer, R. *Feedback Toolkit*. Portland, OR: Productivity Press, 1994.

Maxwell. J. *Developing the Leader Within You*. Nashville,TN: Nelson, 1993.

Nadler, D. *Feedback and Organizational Development*. Reading, MA: Addison-Wesley, 1977.

Peters, T. and R. Waterman. *In Search of Excellence*. New York: Random House, 1985.

Powers, B. *Instructor Excellence*. San Francisco, CA: Jossey-Boss, 1992,

Richardson, B. and M. A. Fusco. *The +10 Percent Principle: How to Get Extraordinary Results from Ordinary People*. San Diego, CA: Pfeiffer and Company, 1993.

Roberts, W. *Leadership Secrets of Attila The Hun*. New York: Warner Books, 1987.

Thomas, P. *Advanced Psycho Cybernetics*. New York: Putnam, 1992.

Chapter 6

Leadership and Management

Executive Summary

If Mark Twain were a worker in a modern organization, he might quip, "Everybody talks about quality, but nobody does anything about it." Although this apocryphal quote is somewhat exaggerated, it is partially–and painfully–true. At least, much of what people have done about quality has been incompletely planned and inconsistently applied.

Many organizations of all types have attempted to jump on the "quality" bandwagon, with widely varying results. One reason why some quality programs fail is that the leaders and managers within the organization do not fully understand the interdependence of leadership and management and the indispensable contributions both must make for true quality to result. And this understanding does not come easily or always predictably. But an understanding of this leadership and management duality is critical to twenty-first century organizational success. Its inherent understanding will be characterized by increased challenges, responsibility, autonomy, risk, and uncertainty. Running an organization with good leadership but without effective management is like trying to find a certain street address by using the best available map of the entire nation. Conversely, trying to run an organization with poor leadership, even if excellent managers are dutifully at work, is akin to attempting a lunar mission launch by using an AAA trip guide. In either situation, the "quality" bandwagon is a rapidly moving target—people who try to jump aboard often cannot catch up or fall off and hurt themselves and others in the process. The result is an understandable but misplaced disillusionment with the entire "quality" movement.

The purpose of this chapter is to present a model for use in conceptualizing the interlocking nature of leadership and management and the tools both must bring to the quality process. A deceptively simple grid chart, which we call the Quality Quadrants, will serve as the vehicle for analyzing this vital, yet often overlooked, principle. The authors hope that the Quality Quadrants will help leaders and managers understand the cooperative nature of quality and the complementary roles each must play. Properly understood, the Quality Quadrants should help leaders and managers at all levels to practically implement key concepts that will yield tangible benefits for all concerned.

Discussion

Leadership and Management Duality

Entire library shelves full of thick books have been written on the subjects of leadership and management. Although the two concepts are often addressed as if they were entirely separate, a person may function as both a leader and a manager, as we mentioned in the first two chapters of this book. Leadership and management fit more neatly in the category of function than an innate birthright status and thus can properly be viewed as two hats, which in some instances may belong to the same individual and worn as the occasion or the job requires. However, usually a given person will spend a preponderance of time in one of the two modes, depending primarily on the individual's official position but also to some extent on personality traits, preferences, and the mix of abilities within the organization.

For purposes of this chapter, we will reduce these two concepts to their most concise, sound-bite, bumper-sticker, fortune-cookie form, while acknowledging the enormous complexity that is subsumed within these short summaries. Specifically, we will distill leadership to "Doing the right thing" while management is "Doing things right." We will briefly discuss each in turn, leaving in-depth analysis to the groaning shelves crammed with fat volumes on each subject in the local library.

Leadership: Doing the Right Things

We can operationally define leadership as influencing the behavior of others toward goal accomplishment. Leadership is an effectiveness-based concept of "Doing the right things."

The leader's role is primarily a strategic one. The leader must set the overall tone for the organizational culture, the very environment in which everyone will operate and which pervades all aspects of the organization's work. The leader's role in shaping the vision and the mission, and the statements which express them, is essential in this regard, since the vision and the mission serve as the beacons for all focused energies and activities. Indeed, the vision and mission are sometimes collectively called the strategic direction in recognition of their overarching effect on guiding all other facets of the operation toward the "right things," whatever those may be, for any given organization at any given point in time.

Within these broad parameters, the leader also will focus the organizational direction on a somewhat more specific level, setting course for one or more desired goals and objectives and providing some system of priorities. Finally, the most pragmatic, quasi-managerial aspect of a leader's role is to oversee formulation of a plan of action that begins to move goals and objectives off the "Flatland" of the drawing board and into the three-dimensional real world of actual activity. All of these more detailed functions grow out of the overall strategic direction and channel efforts more directly toward "doing the right things."

In today's environment leaders increasingly operate in the realm of intangibles, ambiguity, and uncertainty. Determining the "right things" for the people to drive toward, and how generally to set about "doing" them, is an ineffable enterprise to a large extent. The ability to envision the future, to inspire, to motivate, to build confidence, to encourage, or any of the other vital yet elusive aspects of leadership is very difficult to measure directly. The indirect indicia of such traits will be very much in evidence among people in the organization in a host of manifestations, but the quality of effective leadership itself belongs to a higher plane. Leadership supplies the spirit, the animating life-force of an organization. An organization with good leadership is like a living person, with one mind and soul. Thus, leaders are "meaning makers" because they give an organization a sense of purpose and direction. Without it, the organization is more akin to a partially disassembled robot with various sub-components churning and spinning autonomously, lifelessly, mindlessly, and purposelessly. It is for this reason that effective leaders are open to creativity and change and that tomorrow's leaders must live by a simple credo: it's better to steadily learn than to be organizationally dead. Within this context, leaders give people something to believe in. The hallmark of this type of leader is to motivate and inspire their people to accomplish a goal.

This emphasis on the leader's vital role does not mean to imply that the leader does all of this unilaterally and is in isolation from all others within the organization. To the contrary, one of the cardinal virtues a leader must possess is the ability to work with people and draw out their best efforts, ideas, and creativity. The leader must involve everyone at all levels in the strategic planning process of formulating, refining, and implementing the organization's values, vision, mission, goals, objectives, tasks to be accomplished, and plans of action. Properly done, this type of leadership will produce genuine synergy as the combined efforts of a diverse group of people generate far more superior results to those that could ever come from the leader alone or from any other organization subset. Only by orchestrating such combined, focused teamwork can a leader truly spearhead an effective drive to "do the right things."

Management: Doing Things Right

We can operationally define management as controlling and integrating resources to accomplish organizational goals. Management is also an efficiency-based concept of "doing things right."

If leadership deals with the strategic level, then management is concerned with the tactical realm. Tactics are the detail work, the nuts-and-bolts pragmatic enterprises that occupy the most time of the most people in any organization or what would usually be considered the actual job. Management involves taking these activities and organizing them for maximum efficiency and productivity or, in other words, "doing things right."

The manager is sometimes derided as a "bean counter," someone who walks around with a clipboard and a calculator to monitor and meddle in the work of those people who actually produce useful output. This is perhaps an unfair caricature of a manager–particularly a good manager.

A good manager will ensure that everything is operating optimally; the manager will become involved at a level of detail sufficiently precise to allow confirmation that things are indeed going well without "micromanaging" the workers to death. The manager will need to gather and transmit information so this can happen. This entails giving and receiving regular and frequent feedback, both with external and internal customers. The manager needs to have open, two-way lines of communication with all who deal with the organization from the outside and with those people who make it all happen inside the organization. Only through judicious use of such freely flowing information can a manager be equipped to make correct decisions on how to "do things right," i.e., to do the work faster, more economically, and better.

All the raw data in the world will not produce the "faster, cheaper, better" result unless it is effectively organized, analyzed, and channeled into useful actions. This is where metrics come in. Metrics are nothing more than meaningful measures. Metrics take one or more aspects of a process and provide a snapshot for the manager to study. They measure speed, accuracy, customer satisfaction, quantity, frequency of defects, and various other facets of any given process. The manager's job is to ensure that the metrics are aimed at things within the organization's control that are of importance to some aspect of the organization's function and then to use the resulting statistics in a positive, productive way to spur beneficial change. A good manager does not use metrics just for the sake of doing so as if they had the talismanic effect of a potent good-luck charm or the power to protect the manager from evil forces as a garland of garlic might ward off vampires. Metrics foster process understanding and motivate action to continually improve the way we do business and conduct our affairs. The only proper justification for a metric's existence is a demonstrable value added in helping the workers "do things right" consistent with strategic direction provided by the leadership.

Just as a leader does not operate in a vacuum, no manager can function effectively without involving all of the people available. Managers must elicit new ideas and suggestions for positive change and then help make good ideas a reality. Managers should ensure that everyone participates in the formulating and implementing methods of obtaining and using feedback as well as in selecting or modifying metrics and their use. This type of participative management will result in synergistic effects better than anything the best manager could produce alone. It will also foster greater commitment from all workers than the fanciest, most expensive management system imposed by executive fiat from the top down. Truly, no manager is an island. Any manager who wishes to try the "island method" is apt to require frequent rescue attempts similar to the hapless crew of the *Minnow* of "Gilligan's Island" fame.

The Quality Quadrants

This very brief overview of the functions of leadership and management serves to introduce the Quality Quadrants. Similar quadrants will be familiar to most readers, from a variety of contexts, because quadrants are a helpful tool in visualizing the interrelationships between factors. They certainly do not capture the sum total of all existing complexities, but they do serve a useful function by facilitating the understanding of such interactions, at least on a broad conceptual level.

As shown in Figure 1, the Quality Quadrants depict the four basic ways in which leadership and management may interact in any given situation or organization. The horizontal axis takes the concept of leadership, as condensed to its core meaning, and divides it into two very broad categories, i.e., "Doing Right Things," and its evil twin, "Doing Wrong Things." The vertical axis does the same for the management concept, with the managerial universe thereby split into the two polar opposites, "Doing Things Right" and "Doing Things Wrong."

There is obviously no bright line dividing either leadership or management into such clearly separate binary categories in the real world. It is often unclear, even in retrospect, whether a given course of action is "right" for a leader. Ambiguities also exist as to the optimal managerial measures, and "right" or "wrong" is many times a subjective judgment call, heavily influenced by the eye of the beholder. The idea here is not to presume to judge the correctness or wisdom of any particular decision or action. Rather, the question is whether all or most of the effective leadership or management concepts are being used most of the time, as previously discussed. It is the process as a whole that is in issue.

Acknowledging that demarcation lines are often quite blurred, we can nonetheless profit from analysis of the ways in which the two primary leadership and management categories interact in each of the four quadrants. Figure 2 illustrates some specific consequences of combining leadership and management types.

In either Figure, the following overall results are apparent. Quadrant I is "Doing Right Things Right;" Quadrant II is "Doing Wrong Things Right;" Quadrant III is "Doing Right Things Wrong;" and Quadrant IV is "Doing Wrong Things Wrong." We will now examine each of these in turn.

Quadrant I: Doing Right Things Right

This is the felicitous result when both leadership and management are generally on target. Such a happy confluence of strategic and tactical principles is not merely the stuff of myth confined to the early halcyon days of Camelot and other utopias. It can and does happen in reality; if it did not, there would be no point to studying either leadership or management with an eye toward practical dividends.

**LEADERSHIP AND MANAGEMENT
QUALITY QUADRANTS**

Leadership
(Strategic: What You Do)

	Doing Right Things	**Doing Wrong Things**
Doing Things Right	I. Doing Right Things Right	II. Doing Wrong Things Right
Doing Things Wrong	III. Doing Right Things Wrong	IV. Doing Wrong Things Wrong

Management
(Tactical: How You Do It)

FIGURE 1

LEADERSHIP AND MANAGEMENT QUALITY QUADRANTS

Leadership
(Strategic: What You Do)

	Doing Right Things	Doing Wrong Things
	I.	**II.**
Doing Things Right	**LEADERSHIP:** -Cooperative development of Strategic Direction -Vision and Mission with grassroots buy-in -Goals, Objectives, and Plans of Action aligned -All focused on/responsive to genuine needs **DOING RIGHT THINGS RIGHT** **MANAGEMENT:** -Metrics aimed at meaningful factors -Metrics used to drive positive change -Feedback system for external/internal customers -Feedback results used to drive positive change	**LEADERSHIP:** -Strategic Direction absent/no vision of future -Strategic direction imposed/no grassroots buy-in -Goals, Objectives, Plans of Action absent -Goals, Objectives, Plans of Action not aligned **DOING WRONG THINGS RIGHT** **MANAGEMENT:** -Metrics aimed at meaningful factors -Metrics used to drive positive change -Feedback system for external/internal customers -Feedback results used to drive positive changes
	III.	**IV.**
Doing Things Wrong	**LEADERSHIP:** -Cooperative development of Strategic Direction -Vision and Mission with grassroots buy-in -Goals, Objectives, and Plans of Action aligned -All focused on/responsive to genuine needs **DOING RIGHT THINGS WRONG** **MANAGEMENT:** -Metrics absent or aimed at irrelevancies -Metrics not used productively or not used at all -Feedback system absent/asks random questions -Feedback results used to harm/not used at all	**LEADERSHIP:** -Strategic Direction absent/no vision of future -Strategic Direction imposed/no grassroots buy-in -Goals, Objectives, Plans of Action absent -Goals, Objectives, Plans of Action not aligned **DOING WRONG THINGS WRONG** **MANAGEMENT:** -Metrics absent or aimed at irrelevancies -Metrics not used productively or not used at all -Feedback system absent/asks random questions -Feedback results used to harm/not used at all

Management (Tactical: How You Do It)

FIGURE 2

In a Quadrant I situation, the leader has steered the people toward a vision and mission which they all share in common. Within this broad strategic direction, there are more specific goals, and within each goal there is likewise more precise focus on the tangible objectives that comprise ways to attain portions of the goal. At the most practical level, the leader has oriented and inspired the people to devote their best efforts to developing and implementing one or more plans of action in furtherance of each goal and objective. The leader has also led the people to create a priority ranking system so the most significant and/or most important plans of action receive the lion's share of the attention, or are tackled first. The distinguishing feature in Quadrant I is the display of a stalwart balance of both leadership and management. All of this must be aimed at meeting or exceeding genuine, legitimate needs of external or internal customers.

Most important, the leader has succeeded in establishing an organizational culture in harmony with the vision of where the organization should be heading and the mission it is intended to perform. Without this strategic direction, none of the rest would be very effective at achieving meaningful results.

Given that good leadership has brought the organization to the point of "Doing the Right Things," it then falls to management to effectively put all of these good intentions to work. Good management is what will make leadership's strategic direction a tactical, pragmatic success.

To do things right, management must have a system for collecting and processing information, both in terms of regular feedback from external and internal customers and in terms of metrics to gauge performance. The key to having a Quadrant I organization is for this feedback and metrics system to be in alignment with all aspects of the strategic direction. The vision, mission, goals, objectives and plans of action must not only be internally consistent but also supported by a consonant information gathering and analysis mechanism. If there is a disconnect, the system will break down because a constant influx of the right information blend is the fuel that drives the strategic direction engine.

In a Quadrant I organization, the metrics are not merely window-dressing but are actually a useful tool for effectively assessing various phases of the operation. They measure things that really matter to the organization, with the option to change if need be. This means that metrics are not created and used just because something is capable of being measured; metrics are only properly used to evaluate, support, and advance an organization's vision, mission, goals, objectives, or plan of action. Anything else is useless eyewash. Actual use of a metric's information is also essential if the metric is to have real value. The data any metric collects must be actively analyzed and discussed and must serve as the fodder for action initiatives designed to improve whatever process the metric addresses.

Similarly, the feedback system in a Quadrant I organization is not simply an off-the-shelf generic customer satisfaction form but rather is tailored to the specific organization's mission and focused on one or more goals and objectives within that mission. For external customers, the system looks at how well key aspects of the organization's plan of action are being implemented. For internal customers, the system affirmatively seeks ideas and innovations that will improve performance and enhance organizational culture in ways that will support the strategic direction. If something is not important enough to be included in a goal, objective, or plan of action, it probably has no place in a feedback form.

A true Quadrant I organization is more than simply the sum of the best parts of a Quadrant II and a Quadrant III situation melded together into a "greatest hits" collection. There is synergistic interaction between good leadership and effective management in which each feeds the other and carries the overall organization to a higher level than either could alone. This is to be expected, given the necessity for strategic direction to be aimed at genuine, valid, real-world customer need and the importance of aligning all managerial phases of an operation so as to be pointed at the strategic direction. Advancements in either leadership or management will find an able complementary partner ready and waiting to take improvement to the next level because both leadership and management are "right." This is an advantage any Quadrant I organization has over even the best of its Quadrant II or III cousins.

The metrics and feedback structure together form the central nervous system of a Quadrant I organization's information-processing mechanism, supported by and in support of the backbone, the strategic direction. The idea of becoming more efficient, of doing things faster, cheaper, and better, is as old as humanity itself. But the well-planned, intelligent meshing of good leadership and effective management enlivens the idea and ensures that all activity is on target. By obtaining and analyzing relevant bits of information, consistent with and in furtherance of the very reason the organization exists, any group of people can prepare themselves to "Do Right Things Right."

Quadrant II: Doing Wrong Things Right

By "Doing Wrong Things Right," we mean a situation where the operation is "efficient," running smoothly, with adequate charts, graphs, and slogans but where there is no true strategic direction. This is in some respects the worst of all the quadrants because it gives the illusion that all is well, while camouflaging problems that go to the very core. The cliche´ "rearranging deck chairs on the Titanic" is an apt summation of this situation.

An organization can very easily find itself in Quadrant II. Bureaucratic inertia can cause a system to go on autopilot. Tradition, the ways things have always been done, and the comfort people derive from familiar routines all feed the autopilot juggernaut. People from management on down may routinely assume the organization is headed in the right direction because the opposite conclusion simply is unthinkable . . . so no one thinks about it. Essentially, the key characteristics in Quadrant II are ineffective leadership and resolute management.

A Quadrant II organization has not necessarily ignored the "quality" movement and slapped on blinders. Instead, it may be that the leaders and managers have attempted to graft the outward quality manifestations onto their organization but without attending to the type of true inside-out transformations that need to happen for real quality to take hold. Management may have what were once called "efficiency experts" busily keeping track of numerous aspects of the enterprise, counting beans very diligently and calling this metrics. Managers may be doing a wonderful job of making their parts of the system run efficiently and may even have genuine success stories to tell from the limited perspective of their piece of the puzzle. But irrespective of how efficiently these various subcomponents are humming along, the overall organization is in deep trouble.

When leadership fails to lead, systemic paralysis sets in. Despite the fact that the organization may have something called a vision, a mission statement, and other quality decorations prominently on display on the walls, it has no true strategic direction. A handsomely bound strategic plan may exist, but like Brigadoon, only see the light of day once every hundred years. There is no real vision that guides and motivates everyone toward a common future desired state; at most, there is something misleadingly called a vision but without the power thereof. Because the vision is lacking, any existing goals or objectives or initiatives are not unified in support of an overarching, coordinated effort. Haphazard, disjointed attempts to improve may pull in different and even opposing directions. The beehive of activity and efficiency that exists at the managerial level is in actuality a perpetual motion machine that is either running in place or drifting along a random walk.

No one intends to create a Quadrant II situation. It just happens when leaders fail to grasp what quality really means. Leaders may write a vision or mission statement themselves, then present it as an edict to their people as if it came down from Mount Sinai or emerged fully formed from a burning bush and expect them to worship it accordingly. They may even try to involve the people in the process of drafting goals and objectives and plans of action, but something is missing. Somehow, these documents never make it to the implementation phase, or the leaders fail to obtain genuine buy-in from the people who can make or break an organization–the actual workers. People resent what they perceive as hypocrisy at worst or a meaningless time-wasting formality at best, and so the organization's strategic direction initiatives are stillborn. Lofty statements adorn the walls, ambitious plans fill the file cabinets till they bulge, but nothing changes where it really matters.

The result is a deadly illusion. The Quadrant II organization has the superficial appearance of excellence, but beneath this veneer is a system without a soul. The most effective management in the world will not keep an organization afloat for long with inadequate leadership. The worst of it is that because of the outward signs of quality, no one may recognize the underlying decay until it is too late. That is where the Quality Quadrants can play a vital role in identifying hazards such as a Quadrant II situation and spurring the leaders to action before the problems become insurmountable.

Quadrant III: Doing Right Things Wrong

A Quadrant III organization is most likely in the early phases of its quality journey, either because it only recently began the process or because it is stuck in a state of arrested development. Its leadership has set forth a viable strategic direction but this has not been reinforced with effective management at the action level, where the rubric meets the road map. Thus, it is "Doing the Right Things," but it is doing them wrong. Quadrant III is characterized by good leadership but lacks appropriate managerial skills and/or their application.

A great general can do much to lead the troops to victory, but without subordinate commanders who are in tune with the strategy and capable of engineering effective supporting tactics, the ultimate triumph may prove elusive. As with Quadrant II, when either leadership or management is lacking, the result will be both disappointing and predictable.

In a Quadrant III situation, the leader has the overall organization focused on "Doing the Right Things." With true involvement of the people at all levels and commitment from them and the leader to set sail (in unity) for a desirable future state, a viable strategic direction is in place. There may even be supporting goals, objectives, and plans of action, all aligned with the vision and mission. But again, something vital is missing. An essential ingredient, necessary to move all of this strategic direction into the realm of tactical application has been omitted.

Again, there may be the outward appearance that all is well. Management may have metrics in place and may have customer feedback forms available. In today's environment, it is rare for an organization to be so old-fashioned as not to have something along these lines. The problem that throws some organizations into Quadrant III rather than Quadrant I is that these tools are used for the wrong things or are not used at all.

In the area of metrics, management may indeed have bean counters hard at work, but they are counting refried beans. For the sake of having metrics, the managers may have gone after the low-hanging fruit (or beans) and simply measured those aspects of their activities that readily tend themselves to quantitative analysis without regard for whether the metrics actually yield useful–and usable–information. Many times, managers will measure the speed with which something happens without considering whether this is something their customer or anyone else really values, especially if speed comes at the expense of accuracy or freedom from defects. When speed is the primary focus of the metrics, any action driven by analysis of those metrics will inevitably be aimed at making the process faster, which again may result in degradation in quality, responsiveness to the customer's true needs, and other less measurable but more important considerations. To paraphrase a cliche´, "Be careful what you measure; you might change it."

A second managerial problem is not using already available metrics or feedback tools. An organization might have perfectly good metrics and methods of assessing customer satisfaction, but if the managers do not use the information these tools generate, or use it improperly, the tools are useless, at best. Often information is harvested in great abundance, only to be left to lie in the fields, or files. Numbers are collected and crunched, but nothing ever happens to the mangled figures other than to be given a decent burial deep within a filing cabinet never to rise again. This is what happens when metrics are forced from above on an organization, without buy-in from the front-line managers. They dutifully gather and report the data, but that ends the process as far as they or their workers are concerned. Alternatively, well-intentioned but misguided managers may use the numbers as a weapon with which to punish workers for what is perceived as poor performance. Predictably, the number-whipped workers will despise the entire process and will have little or no allegiance to the strategic direction under which the system arose, regardless of how good the overall leadership might be.

An effective system of internal customer feedback would detect such problems and give managers a chance to correct them. Unfortunately, the same conditions that led to the Quadrant III situation, i.e., bad or improperly used metrics and feedback mechanisms, are apt to preclude management from obtaining or using this key information. The workers– the internal customers–would in all likelihood be acutely aware of any number of problems, including inadequate training, inequitable distribution of work, unclear direction, duplication of effort, poor priority setting, and many others. However, without a workable system for management to tap into this resource, the managers will remain oblivious to it, similar to a landowner who dozes, unaware of the vast fortune in oil gurgling inches beneath the roots of the shade trees that hold his comfortable hammock.

If the leaders and managers of such an organization perform an honest self-check using the Quality Quadrants, they should discover the problem. They might have been puzzled and disappointed by their failure to see much in the way of rewards from all the effort they had poured into their quality program. Indeed, some may have decided that quality does not work and does more harm than good by taking time away from "productive" work. The truth–that the difficulty has been in the implementation at the tactical/managerial level– may be unpleasant, but at least Quality Quadrant analysis will give the people in charge the opportunity to do something to fix it.

Quadrant IV: Doing Wrong Things Wrong

In a Quadrant IV situation, both leadership and management are ineffective. Although the obvious conclusion is that this is the worst situation of all, it may be that here, unlike some Quadrant II and III organizations, the problems are so obviously serious that someone somewhere will realize it and take the necessary corrective actions. On the other hand, just as in many Quadrant II and III situations, a Quadrant IV organization may have the appearance, but not the reality, of effective leadership and management. In that event, Quadrant IV truly is the quality equivalent of the seventh level of Dante's Inferno. Quadrant IV demonstrates a clear lack of both leadership and management

When an organization is "Doing Wrong Things Wrong," its leaders are failing to set forth persuasively–or inspirationally–a strategic direction that points everyone in the right orientation. Either there are no vision, mission, goals, objectives, and/or plans of action, or they were developed without meaningfully involving the whole organization and securing grassroots commitment throughout the process. The resulting organization drift subjects the entire enterprise to the perils of random motion, or no motion at all–bureaucratic paralysis.

The situation is no better on the management side. The information gathering/processing system is either nonexistent or, more likely, ineffective. Whatever metrics exist are aimed at suboptimal targets, or the data are not used to improve worthwhile processes. The feedback system for external and internal customers is not asking the right questions, or maybe the managers are not doing anything productive with the answers. Consequently, myriad problems relating to inefficiency and ineptitude haunt the system with management having no effective means of hunting them down and exercising them. Managerial actions tend to be sporadic, uncoordinated, and even counterproductive–punishing people for things beyond their control.

A Quadrant IV situation is probably worse in both the leadership and management sides than the typical Quadrant II or III organization is in either aspect. This is because a type of negative synergy can prevail where both leadership and management are off-track. Again, there is no unfathomable gulf between leadership and management; there is spillover, and each has an effect on the other. In a Quadrant II situation, effective management might to some degree prop up faulty leadership and fill in some of the gaps left by the errant leaders. Similarly, a Quadrant III organization's viable leadership might trickle down to the action level and partially compensate for erratic management. There is no such lifeline available when an organization finds itself in Quadrant IV. It may be such a case that spawned the concept of "the blind leading the blind."

Would the leaders and managers of such an organization be able to recognize the problems through use of the Quality Quadrants? The answer depends on whether their failings stem from hopeless incompetence or from ignorance and misunderstanding. The former, while certainly possible, is unlikely to exist for very long in any organization, whether in the private or public sector; the pressures of competition and/or the inevitability of independent evaluation from above will eventually root out the truly inept. The latter is far more probable and leaves open the hope that objective self-examination will let the leaders and managers see themselves in Quadrant IV when they look at themselves in the Quality Quadrant mirror.

Conclusion

Whatever an organization's current state, it is useful for the leaders and managers to take a hard look at themselves through the lens of the Quality Quadrants. If nothing else, it is worthwhile to have a practical reminder of what leadership and management should be doing in a healthy organization. It should also prove instructive to focus on the nexus between leadership and management—to gain a deeper appreciation of the importance of both, working together synergistically, to the overall success of the entire enterprise.

People sometimes become so engrossed in their own work that they fail to grasp the web of interlocking relationships of which they are only one part. Leaders and managers, because of their relatively high status within a given hierarchy, may be especially prone to this brand of myopia. The Quality Quadrants, however, teach us that no leader or manager, no matter how brilliant, can single-handedly create or maintain a topnotch organization. Each needs the complementary contributions of the other in order to achieve the highest degrees of success.

In sum, the effective application of the Quality Quadrants will help us to better understand that all change is not progress and that all movement is not forward. The model we have presented is intended to help those involved in leadership and management to simply accomplish their goals a little better.

Discussion Questions and Ideas

- Describe the significant distinguishing characteristics of a person in each of the quality quadrants:

  Quadrant I: Doing Right Things Right
  Quadrant II: Doing Wrong Things Right
  Quadrant III: Doing Right Things Wrong
  Quadrant IV: Doing Wrong Things Wrong

- In what quadrant would you place yourself? Why? Is this where you want to be? If not, where would you rather be? Why? How can you best get there?

- In what quadrant would you place your boss? Why? What can you learn from your boss's example and experience?

- Within your organization, analyze and give some specific examples of each of the four Quality Quadrants cited in this chapter.

• Explain why some people are in either Quadrant II, III, or IV? Why are not more people in Quadrant I? What specific action can be taken to cause leaders and managers to demonstrate Quadrant I behaviors?

• Can the Quality Quadrant concept be applied to nations as well as individuals and organizations? If so, how would you categorize the United States at various key junctures of history? Where would you place some other nations of the world today?

Bibliography and Recommended Reading

Abramson, Mark A. "In Search of the New Leadership." *Government Executive.* September 1996.

Bennis, Warren. *On Becoming a Leader.* Illinois: Austin Press and Erwin, Inc.,1995.

Champy, James and Nitin Nohria. *Fast Forward.* Boston: Harvard Business School Press, 1996.

Creech, Bill. *The Five Pillars of TQM.* New York: Plume/Penguin, 1994.

Department of the Air Force, Headquarters Air Force Systems Command. *The Metrics Handbook.* Andrews Air Force Base, D.C., 1991.

Hammer, Michael and Steven Stanton. *The Reengineering Revolution.* New York: Harper Collins, 1995.

Hersey, Paul; Kenneth H.Blanchard: and Dewey E. Johnson, *Management of Organization Behavior.* Upper Saddle River: NJ.: Prentice Hall, 1996.

Kotter, John P. *Change.* Boston: Harvard Business School Press, 1996.

Ibid: Interview by Richard Lester and Randy Wooten. Harvard Business School, Ibid: *The New Rules.* New York: Free Press, 1995. Cambridge: MA.: 28 June 1993.

Peters, Tom. *The Pursuit of WOW!* New York: Vintage, 1994.

Tee, Andrew. "Editorial." *Synergy: Management Journal, Ministry of Defense,* Singapore, November 1995.

Chapter 7

Using the Law for Competitive Leadership Advantage

Executive Summary

Leaders who have significant problems caused by failure to know or abide by the law will lose the survival game. It is essential for leaders to know which areas of the law are most applicable to them and how the law affects their organization. Discrimination, sexual harassment, environmental issues, and using an office computer for improper purposes are all examples of how the law can impact the survival leader. These and other related legal issues are addressed in this chapter.

Discussion

Law for Leaders–Who Needs It?

In this book, we have covered a wide variety of topics that are relevant to the success or failure of a person as a leader. There remains, however, one more area to discuss. This is a subject that, if ignored, can absolutely destroy everything a leader has accomplished.

To be truly effective, a leader must be aware of the law, must obey the law, and must be perceived by others as obeying the law. The example of President William Jefferson Clinton immediately comes to mind. Although public opinion polls have shown that many Americans believe he did a good job as president, the widely publicized scandals that plagued his administration caused him serious personal and political damage. In effect, his positive achievements have been overshadowed by legal controversies, and his legacy has been seriously undermined.

If a leader is to be able to inspire and mentor, over and above the management of tangible projects, he or she must, at a minimum, be law abiding. This is the floor, not the ceiling. In addition to the actuality of propriety, it is important that the leader be seen as a person of integrity who respects the law. If the leader is perceived as a seeker of loopholes, a limits stretcher who walks the uncertain line between legality and illegality, or a hair-splitting semantic wizard who depends on fine nuances and legalistic definitional gymnastics to avoid liability, that perception will infect the entire organization and all those who deal with it. The effect will be both negative and significant.

Obeying the law is not an easy or simple matter. One reason there are so many lawyers today is that there is a bewildering, expanding, evolving, and complex web of statutes, regulations, and court cases that can cause even the most well-intentioned leader to wonder what the law requires in some circumstances.

Laypersons may assume that "The Law" is a clearly defined set of rules that can easily be discovered by simply looking in a reference book. But law is not like math. Very little is clear and unambiguous. For one thing, judges at various levels, and in both state and federal courts, interpret the Constitution and all statutory and regulatory law. The resulting "common law" decisions often feature interpretations of the law that vary from jurisdiction to jurisdiction and change over time. Additionally, there may be layer upon layer of applicable statutes and regulations at the federal, state, and municipal level in some subject matter areas, all of which must be obeyed. Even for the codified "black letter" law of statutes and regulations within each level of jurisdiction, it can be quite difficult to understand the densely worded, exception filled language.

It is not easy even for experienced attorneys to determine what the law requires in some situations. Three years of intensive study in law school, followed by years of practical experience, are not always enough to enable a lawyer to cut through the legal thicket. Therefore, a non-lawyer must be willing to consult expert legal counsel for help in successfully steering clear of the hazards of the modern world. As is often said on television, "These people are trained professionals; do not attempt this at home." Attempting to cut costs by avoiding legal help is a very dangerous way to save money. The old saying declares, "Any lawyer who represents himself has a fool for a client." If that is true for a lawyer (and it is), it goes double for anyone not thoroughly trained in the law. Do not try to do it yourself!

That having been said, it is possible to distill the essence of most legal challenges down to a few simple rules of thumb that at least can let you know when you are in a potential trouble spot. What, then, are the most significant legal pitfalls that can bring down any leader? And what can you do to avoid such self-destruction?

1. Don't Be Stupid

It is astonishing how many successful, well-educated, adult, prosperous, apparently mature leaders ruin their careers and their lives by doing something stupid. Here we are not talking about inadvertently violating some obscure provision of a complex, highly technical regulation. No lawyers are necessary in these cases. We are talking about the kind of things you learned were wrong in kindergarten, junior Sunday School, or in your parents' living room.

What is it that compels grown people to shoplift an inexpensive cassette tape from a K-Mart shelf? What drives senior leaders to steal equipment and supplies from their workplace? What moves mature role models to abuse their spouse or their children? What force impels top-level managers to download pornographic materials from their office computer? What demons spur a boss to make sexual advances to a subordinate in the workplace?

Probably the most important lesson a leader can learn about the law is this. If it seems stupid to do something, he or she should stop right there. Go no further. To put it another way, if you would be ashamed to tell your mother about something you are planning to do, it's likely wrong on either a moral or legal level or both. Resist the temptation and squelch the urge to do something stupid! Your career and your life will be much the better for it.

There are very practical reasons why a leader should obey this rule in addition to the ethical and moral duty we all share. There is a good chance you will get caught if you try to steal from a store or use your office computer to view pornography. Video surveillance cameras and electronically protected merchandise are in widespread use today. It is quite a foolhardy gamble to slip a small item in your pocket under the assumption that no one will notice. And there are very powerful countermeasures routinely used in large organizations today to detect unlawful or unauthorized computer use.

It is entirely possible for supervisors and security personnel to monitor what you are doing with your office computer. From a remote location, other people can see exactly what you see on your computer screen. They can examine, one by one, each website you have accessed. They can check the contents of your hard-drive. They can read your e-mail messages. And they do not need a search warrant to do so. If you visit pornographic websites or swap inappropriate e-mail messages from your office computer, don't be surprised if someone else on your Local Area Network is right there with you, invisible to you, noting your every (stupid) move!

Odds are, you did not become a leader because you are stupid. On the contrary, you have probably risen to your current position because you have a fair amount of intelligence and common sense. Don't check your brains and your common sense at the door when you embark on leisure pursuits, whether in the workplace or outside.

2. Don't Discriminate

To some extent, this overlaps rule number one. Many instances of illegal discrimination are so blatantly, obviously wrong that a person would be stupid to think they were permissible. However, there are several federal statutes that govern discrimination, and the requirements are so sufficiently complex that a leader should consult the services of an experienced attorney from time to time.

Discrimination on the basis of race, sex, age, religion, or national origin is, to oversimplify a complicated subject, unlawful. Title VII of the Civil Rights Act is one of the most far-reaching federal laws in this area. The Americans with Disabilities Act is another powerful, if more recent, federal anti-discrimination statute. These statutes have been interpreted by various federal courts, resulting in an array of clarifications, refinements, and definitions.

This is not an easy area. It is not necessarily safest merely to bend over backward to favor historically oppressed minorities. Recent federal judicial decisions and legislation in some states have placed the legality of affirmative action in doubt. Yet it is also risky to make all business decisions on a category-blind, purely merit basis, giving no consideration to the "disparate impact" this might have on, for example, the number and salaries of women or minorities in certain positions.

If a leader makes the wrong decisions here, even in good faith and with the best of intentions, the consequences can be disastrous. Even informal allegations of bias and bigotry can poison a leader's relationships with his or her own people as well as outsider observers. Formal administrative complaints or actual litigation can also result. This is most emphatically not something to be taken for granted or handled on the fly.

Violations can be large or small, but all violations are dangerous to a leader. Relatively innocuous activities such as telling or tolerating "jokes" of a racial or sexual nature can be unlawful and certainly can undermine a leader's moral authority to lead. Leaders must also be alert for subtle discrimination in the form of stereotypically limiting people to certain types of duties on the basis of their race or sex. And remember, as society is different now from what it was thirty years ago, so too has the law evolved. What might have been acceptable at one time may well be unlawful today.

3. Don't Cheat

When bedeviled by a host of difficult, demanding, costly legal rules and regulations, a leader can be tempted to cut a few corners. This is especially true where the law seems to make no sense and where little if any benefit is perceived as flowing from compliance with the law. There is a real burden in complying with the law in terms of both actual expense and lost opportunity costs. Why not cheat a little and save some money?

Two of the primary areas in which cheating can lure the unwary into deep trouble are environmental law and tax law. Both of these are extraordinarily complex topics which pose great challenges even to those who work in the field full-time. It is a formidable task to determine what is required, let alone to do what is required. Both cost a lot of money and may yield little, if any, obvious, tangible benefit to those who pay the costs of compliance. At some level, it can appear to be a "victimless crime" to violate the law in either area. Who is harmed if a person or a corporation pays a little less tax than the IRS says it wants? Who gets hurt if a firm's environmental record-keeping and reporting are not exactly perfect?

Well, to put it bluntly, you do. If you get caught in your cheating, there are stiff civil and criminal penalties awaiting you. And even if you don't get caught by the authorities, the people within your organization who know about your illegal activities will think less of you. This will likely spread over time, undermining your ability to lead and to mentor. Not many people want a mentor like Fagan was to Oliver Twist, i.e., a crook who will teach them how to be crooks too.

There are many other areas in which compliance with the law might seem overly onerous and in which noncompliance might seem easy. Building codes, occupational safety and health requirements, fair labor standards, state and local administrative rules, and myriad other legal hoops bedevil leaders and managers at all levels. But cheating is not the answer, and it never will be.

4. Don't Abuse Your Position

This "thou shalt not" rule blends into some of the others, especially rule number two, but it is sufficiently distinct and dangerous that it warrants separate mention. The cliché "Power corrupts, and absolute power corrupts absolutely" attained the status of a cliché for one very good reason—it is true.

In the military, there is another cliché, "Rank has its privileges." Although this is true, it is very hard for some people to know where to draw the line between accepting the proper fruits of success and corruptly using, and abusing, one's power and position for personal gain. That is because the line is not clear in many circumstances. But leaders sometimes cannot resist the urge to walk that fuzzy, shifting line as if it were a tightrope, hanging high above the hard, cold ground with no safety net in sight.

There are plenty of different ways in which a leader may abuse his or her position, and, human nature being what it is, clever, inventive people are constantly finding new ways to do so. One of the most common problems, however, is sexual harassment.

Sexually-oriented comments and actions that might be acceptable under other circumstances are totally inappropriate and even illegal when a leader is dealing with a subordinate. The Civil Rights Act, and the case law that interprets it, has prohibited various forms of sex discrimination, including sexual harassment. Unlawful sexual harassment itself can take a variety of forms, including "hostile work environment." As with environmental law and tax law, the legal requirements in this area can be challenging to pin down, but it is far better to err on the side of caution than bravado.

The law recognizes that there is a power disparity between any supervisor and his or her subordinates. The supervisor can influence the subordinates' working conditions, perquisites, pay, promotions, career advancement, and continued employment. That gives the supervisor enormous leverage, whether explicit or implicit, in any relationship with a subordinate. They can never be true equals, even outside the workplace and on their own time, because the inescapable fact remains that one of them wields significant power over the other.

The law on sexual harassment generally bars only "unwanted" or "unwelcome" sexual advances. But where a supervisor and subordinate are involved, their inherent power disparity makes it doubtful that there can truly be consent by the subordinate. At some level, the subordinate must always be aware that these sexual comments and actions are coming from his or her boss and that the boss may not take "no" for an answer–at least not without making the subordinate pay a price for saying no. Because of this, it is extremely dangerous for any leader to allow a sexual personal relationship to develop with any subordinate no matter how willing or even aggressively eager the subordinate might appear. At some point, the subordinate may decide to report the relationship, perhaps with embellishments that will be very difficult to refute, and the leader may face formal legal sanctions.

In addition, there can be a profoundly deleterious effect on others within the organization if the boss is even perceived as engaging in a sexual relationship with one of his or her employees. Other subordinates will, quite understandably, fear that the boss's sexual partner will receive special treatment and favors that are denied those who do not engage in such conduct. A fetid atmosphere of favoritism, whether actual or perceived, will permeate the organization. Trust will be destroyed, and suspicion will replace it. Envy and resentment will drive out unity and harmony. The leader cannot be effective under such conditions.

One price a leader pays for being the leader is that he or she forfeits the freedom to deal on a personal level with subordinates as if they were peers. This is not a particularly difficult concept to grasp. Although the exact limits of controlling legal authority may not always be sharply defined, the wise leader will scrupulously avoid even the appearance of impropriety and stay always a safe distance away from any borderline activity. The borderline in these cases is often the edge of a steep and deadly cliff.

Of course, it is also important for leaders to refrain from abusing their authority in other areas as well. Borrowing money from subordinates, asking them to do work "as a favor" for the supervisor personally and other unfair practices are not only lousy leadership techniques but may also be in violation of various labor laws.

One of the most rigorous tests of leadership is the allure of the privileges a leader may be tempted to claim. Such temptations may corrupt a person unless he or she has determined, in advance, to permit no exceptions to the rules.

5. Be Nice to Your "Mother Nature"

We have mentioned the complexity of environmental law and the urge some leaders feel to "cook the books" a bit to save time, money, and effort. This is one of the deadliest traps for the unwary, and here are a few reasons why.

For all intents and purposes, environmental law did not exist until 1969, when the National Environmental Policy Act (NEPA) was enacted, bringing with it the law of Environmental Impact Statements and ushering in the modern era of environmental regulation. Since then, there has been a profusion of major federal statutes and implementing regulations, coupled with numerous state and local versions of these laws. A veritable tidal wave of new laws has flooded the nation, and environmental law has been the fastest growing, fastest changing legal specialty of the past three decades.

The following are some of the most significant federal environmental statutes, listed in no particular order.

(1)   Clean Air Act
(2)   Federal Water Pollution Control Act (Clean Water Act)
(3)   National Environmental Policy Act (NEPA)
(4)   Resource Conservation and Recovery Act (RCRA)
(5)   Endangered Species Act (ESA)

(6) Comprehensive Environmental Response, Compensation, and Liability Act (CERCLA, or Superfund)
(7) Safe Drinking Water Act (SDWA)
(8) Toxic Substances Control Act (TSCA)
(9) Emergency Planning and Community Right to Know Act (EPCRA)
(10) Federal Insecticide, Fungicide, and Rodenticide Act (FIFRA)
(11) Coastal Zone Management Act (CZMA)
(12) Pollution Prevention Act (PPA)
(13) Noise Control Act (NCA)
(14) Oil Pollution Act (OPA)
(15) Marine Mammals Protection Act (MMPA)
(16) Ocean Dumping Act, or Marine Protection, Research, and Sanctuaries Act (MPRSA)
(17) Solid Waste Disposal Act (SWDA)

No one, not even a full-time environmental attorney, can be thoroughly familiar with all of these federal statutes. And the statutes are just the beginning. Federal environmental statutes are implemented by federal regulations, which can be lengthier and more convoluted than the statutes themselves. The federal statutes and regulations are all subject to judicial review at the various levels of federal courts, resulting in case law that refines, modifies, and interprets the "black letter law." Then, the states have a significant role in applying several of the major federal environmental statutes within each state's jurisdiction. As part of this process, many states have passed their own versions of the federal statutes, modifying the focus and tailoring the provisions to fit their local needs. Generally, the states are free to impose stricter environmental controls than provided by the federal law but not more lax controls. The state laws are also interpreted by the courts, leading to further refinements. Finally, municipalities can also regulate certain aspects of environmental activity and in the process create yet another layer of law to learn and obey.

Does your head hurt yet? We have not even discussed the vast number of pages and the degree of complexity, overlap, and contradiction these various laws entail. Nor would it be possible to do so in anything other than a massive, multi-volume, frequently updated legal treatise. As just one example, the 1990 amendments to the Clean Air Act were more than 900 pages long, and these were just the amendments, not the underlying statute, and did not include the voluminous implementing regulations nor the ever-expanding body of case law on point, nor the state versions.

Environmental law can be counterintuitive, exasperating, confusing, and unfair. But these laws have teeth, and those teeth can bite. There are severe civil and criminal penalties associated with violations of these laws. Many of the federal statutes provide for civil fines of $27,500 per day per violation. As the saying goes, pretty soon you're talking about real money. And don't assume that no environmental laws apply to your organization just because you're not a major oil company. These laws reach down to the level of the individual citizen in some cases and can affect us in surprising ways. Bottom line: competent legal advice from an environmental specialist is often one of the best investments a leader can make.

6. Watch Your Mouth

One of the ways in which law for leaders has changed most dramatically during recent years is in the degree to which people can be penalized for jokes and offhand comments. Defamation suits, complaints of racial or sexual bias, allegations of discrimination against the handicapped, and other serious legal consequences can flow from a moment spent flapping one's lips.

Never assume that your comments are "off the record" or private, no matter where you are speaking and no matter how few and how trusted your intended listeners. Circumstances change, people change, and people are not always what they appear to be. It is best to assume that *everything* you say is *on the record* and open to widespread public scrutiny, always.

Maybe at one time leaders could get away with telling "dirty jokes," making racial slurs, using derogatory language in reference to women, making fun of a person's disabilities or physical appearance, deriding someone's sexual orientation, commenting about a person's religious affiliation, or using vulgar language. If there ever was such a time, that time has most definitely passed in America today.

Leaders must be scrupulously just and above reproach. Don't try to test the limits of what you can get away with. Avoid even the appearance of impropriety. Eliminate all negative or slang terms from your vocabulary relating to racial or ethnic groups, gender, sexual orientation, religion, and physical/mental disability. Never tell, tolerate, or circulate a joke that in any way focuses on these topics. The potential for legal damage is too great. Moreover, you can lose respect in the eyes of your colleagues and followers if you fall prey to these mouth-inflicted harms.

7. Play Fair

Leaders must be fair with the people in their employ as well as with the people with whom they do business. One way in which this fundamental moral principle intersects with the law is in the area of contracts.

Many people have an employment contract which sets forth the major terms of their professional relationship with their employer. These terms include salary or wages, working hours, working conditions, various benefits, provisions for promotion or advancement, disciplinary procedures, and avenues for redress of grievances. Some leaders might find certain of these contractual elements bothersome and inconvenient. They may be inclined to ignore or circumvent the offending contractual clauses. They may want to cheat a little around the edges of some rights guaranteed by the contract.

Do not do anything other than abide by the letter and the spirit of each employee's contract. To do otherwise opens you up to an Unfair Labor Practice complaint, a breach of contract lawsuit, a union grievance, and other legal consequences. Plus, once word gets out–and it will–you will suffer greatly in the eyes of your other employees.

When in doubt on a contractual matter, give the benefit of the doubt to your employee. Do not engage in legal hair-splitting over the precise meaning of contract terms. Resist the impulse to locate and exploit loopholes in the contract. Restrain yourself from using the might of your legal team to gain an unfair advantage over your workers. Even if you "win" legally, you lose a lot in terms of your continuing relationship with the employee in question and all your other employees as well.

The same holds true of your contracts with suppliers, customers, sub-contractors, independent contractors, temporary workers, and anyone else with whom you engage in business dealings. You might get away with unfair exploitation of your competitive advantage once or twice and succeed in giving someone less than the contract calls for. You might be able to hide behind an ambiguous contract term to provide less than was bargained for, once or twice. You may win the momentary legal battle and force the other side into an unfavorable out-of-court settlement or even beat them in court on narrow legal grounds. But, again, this is likely to be a Pyrrhic victory. Beware in the future when you have to deal with the people you outsmarted before. They will be ready for you next time. And so will everyone else who hears about your contractual sleight-of-hand. Bad stuff rolls downhill, and you will be in a veritable Death Valley from now on.

Fairness will pay dividends to you. You will avoid plenty of costly, annoying, time-consuming court battles, grievances, and complaints. Your employees and colleagues will respect and trust you. And you will sleep better at night.

No modern leader can afford to ignore the lessons from the recent highly publicized scandals in the corporate world. The core problem in the Enron, WorldCom, Arthur Andersen, and similar debacles is a simple one, albeit clothed in plenty of expensive, sophisticated disguises.

A leader must keep both eyes wide open for conflicts of interest that can poison the honest flow of information and the normal checks on unbridled self-service. If, for example, the same person or organization is hired to be both an independent auditor and a corporate advisor to a given company, this is akin to trusting a chimpanzee with matches and dynamite to be your safety inspector.

Likewise, when CEOs and other top executives stand to reap huge personal gains from stock options in their own companies, there is a powerful impulse to broil the books to exaggerate corporate earnings and paint a misleading picture rosier than a Rose Parade version of the portrait of Dorian Gray. When leaders deceive investors, or allow such deception to happen on their watch, they are also deceiving themselves. They risk criminal sanctions, the bankruptcy of their company, and personal ruination, all for the lure of easy, undeserved money.

Is such corporate fraud, deception, and evidence shredding playing by the rules? Is it being honest? At times, the law is not "black letter," as lawyers say, but instead a bewildering spectrum of shades of Dorian Gray. Accountants, attorneys, and corporate leaders can be sorely tempted to exploit those gray areas in the law to a very aggressive extent in an attempt to derive every possible advantage in today's cutthroat competitive environment. There is a fine and fuzzy line between shrewd business practice and illegality. But in that thicket of gray lurk many career killers. And with Enron et al, the proverbial organic waste matter eventually hits the oscillating air circulation device. The resulting fiasco can move Congress to hurriedly enact new, strict, draconian, and all-too-clear legislation to sew shut any loopholes. So, stay away from the gray!

Leaders must make it clear to their accountants, lawyers, and advisors that no conflicts of interest will be tolerated. And while encouraging zealous pursuit of excellence and success, leaders must make every member of the team understand that the law is to be followed, not run away from. It is not worth it to stretch the envelope of legality. Just ask the former executives, employees, and investors ruined in the recent corporate scandals.

Conclusion

This chapter is not intended to make you a legal expert on any of the pitfalls we have described. Our goal is to make you aware of the traps for the unwary so that you will not be unwary. Your personal reputation, your career, your family, and your organization are all dependent on how you behave in relation to the law's mandates. If you wish to be a survivor, the absolute worst thing you could do is to try to become an armchair lawyer and, armed with a little knowledge, decide to tiptoe around the rim of the bottomless chasm of illegality.

Be smart. Be safe. Stay far away from the danger zones. That is what a survivor would do when it comes to any decision between obeying or breaking the law. There is far too much at stake to do otherwise.

Discussion Questions and Ideas

• Are you aware of any examples of leaders who had significant problems caused by failure to know or abide by the law? How, if at all, did these problems diminish the effectiveness of these leaders?

• What areas of the law are most applicable to you in your profession? Are you satisfied with the legal advice and assistance available to you? If not, what can you do about it?

• Have you ever had a supervisor who appeared to engage in favoritism? How did this affect the organization?

• Have you ever had a supervisor who appeared to engage in discrimination? What was the impact on you? On your co-workers? On the organization?

• Has sexual harassment ever been a problem in any organization to which you belonged? How did this influence the way people related to one another in the organization? How could the situation have been improved?

• Have you ever known a leader whose philosophy regarding legal advice was "Don't ask the question if you can't stand the answer," or "It's easier to get forgiveness than permission"? Was this leader successful? If so, why? If not, why not?

• In your opinion, is it more accurate to describe the lawyers with whom you work as problem solvers or troublemakers? Why?

- To what extent does environmental law affect your professional life? What is the attitude toward environmental law within your organization?

- Have you ever known of a senior leader who got in trouble for committing an offense such as shoplifting or using an office computer for improper purposes? Why do you think this person did such a thing? What do you suppose they were thinking at the time they chose to commit their crime? Did they think of the other people who depend on them? What would you have done?

- If a person is willing to engage in small-scale illegal activities does that in any way affect his or her ability to be an effective leader? Does it matter whether he or she gets caught? Does it matter whether anyone else "gets hurt" by the illegal activities?

Chapter 8

Time Management Techniques for the Survival Leader

Executive Summary

"If you haven't got the time to do it right, when will you find the time to do it over?"

Jeffrey J. Mayer

Time management, as presented in this chapter, is organizing for action. Time is the common denominator in all the chapters we have presented in this book. It takes time to be an effective survival leader. This chapter looks at time wasters and provides valuable tips to help the leader make better use of his or her time, get more done in less time, avoid time traps, and get organized. Mastering time is no task for the faint of heart. If you are among the all too many people in leadership positions who feel overwhelmed, cheer up. Be resolved to make the most of the limited time you have, and if you are willing to pay the price—then study this material carefully. Some real surprises lie ahead.

Discussion

Where Have All the Minutes Gone? Long Time Passing!

Have you ever heard people talk about what they do with their "free time"? Do you, as a busy leader and manager, have enough "free time"? Trick question, sorry. Unfortunately, just as there is no such thing as a free lunch, there is no such thing as free time. All time is valuable, and all time is costly, whether it is spent in play, work, rest, or commuting.

It is tragic how most people fail to think about the tendency for time to slip through their grasp—tragic, but not surprising since time is invisible and intangible, both omnipresent and impossible to capture. But if we do not confront the issue of time leak, we leave ourselves vulnerable to running out of it before we even know what is happening. Time disappears so quickly and stealthily, slipping down an inescapable hole like quicksand in an hourglass. Even five minutes each workday would amount to about 24 over the course of a year. Every minute has value and once lost can never be replaced.

Many leaders and managers are especially susceptible to the peculiar strain of mass delusion that holds that sheer quantity of time spent at work equates to diligence, professionalism, and dedication. If the number of hours passed at work were a good indicator of excellence, every office would use a time clock, and promotions would be determined on the basis of who amassed the most hours physically spent at the workplace. We all know, on some level, that this is not true. But too many of us, nonetheless, live our lives as if more were always better and that time has to come from somewhere. If you now devote 60, 80, 100 hours per week to your work, are all those hours really necessary? Could you more profitably, in the most genuine sense of the word, spend some of that time differently, whether at work or at some other pursuit?

The cliché holds that time is money, and many individuals know this to be true from their personal experiences. They find it very difficult to make or adhere to a budget with either time or money. They seem incapable of grasping how much is available and how much is required for various purposes. As a consequence, people often live their lives the same way they manage their finances, in effect living on the brink of bankruptcy from paycheck to paycheck, as best they can, with no workable system in place to enable them to gain control. How can we make, and keep, a time budget that will free us from this trap of time anarchy? We need to begin by establishing a baseline of how we are currently spending–or wasting–our time.

Establish a Time Budget Baseline

The best way to gauge our current use of time is to keep a detailed log, just as highly paid professionals do in the private sector when they are keeping track of billable hours. Let us take any fairly typical stretch of seven consecutive days and conduct an experiment. Begin on any given workday, and, from the moment you arrive at work (or, better, from the moment you awaken), write down what exactly you do and for how long you do it. This includes chatting with co-workers, making photocopies, faxing, commuting, talking on the phone, everything. Be reasonably precise in terms of how much time you spend doing each activity, too; using a chart broken down into five-minute segments is a good way to track time expenditures, quickly and easily. Then, after a week, your log should reveal some important facets of the way you function at work. The results may be surprising!

We conduct this experience for seven consecutive days for a reason. In addition to tracking work-related activities, an effective leader will also want to monitor the time spent in other aspects of life as well. After all, a leader must maintain balance among the various key facets of life, including time spent with family, with friends, with community or religious activities, and in all the multifarious functions that combine to make up the mosaic of our lives. Sleep, entertainment, reading, exercising, socializing–all have their indispensable role, and all must be allotted a certain portion of our time budget. But unless we occasionally log the amount of time we spend in each activity, we are vulnerable to having some functions parasitize or crowd out others, perhaps without our even being aware it is happening.

Did your one-week look at your time expenditures teach you anything about how you are living your life? Were you disappointed that time devoted to dining with your family was less than that spent attending meetings, commuting, or chatting with other members of your office? Were you expecting to see less time consumed by some activities and more by others?

Let us focus for a moment on one "activity" which consumes a surprising and disproportionately large amount of the time of the average person–watching television. We could just as easily select any number of other examples, but television viewing is such a huge source of time loss for so many people that it may make a more powerful point if we look at it instead of less voracious time-consumers.

Television, the Black Hole of Time

How much time do you spend watching television on a typical day? Many Americans devote an astonishingly large slice of their daily ration of time to this potentially educational and somewhat pleasant but largely passive, unproductive, and unrewarding pursuit. Could some of that time be better spent doing something else? One will never know unless there is an accounting of where the time goes.

Use your log to keep track of how much time you spend, on average, staring at a television screen each day. Then, when you are confident that you have determined a fairly accurate estimate of your typical daily television time, do some simple math. Multiply that daily average by 365 to see the number of hours you are passing in TV-land each year. Then, if you are really bold, multiply your yearly average by whatever you think is a fair approximation of your remaining life expectancy, be it 30 years, 40 years, or some other figure. Take that number and divide by 24 to see how many entire days you are spending in this "activity."

For example, if you are one of those self-disciplined souls who watch only three hours of television per average day–far less than the national average–that adds up to 1095 hours per year. In just one year, that is the equivalent of around-the-clock all-nighter level viewing for over 45 solid days. If you hope to live another 30 years, you can look forward to spending 1,350 days of it–over 3 + entire years–doing nothing more than making eye contact with your television screen. And remember, these are days and years of 24-hours-a-day watching television. If you prefer to think of this in terms of 8-hour workday equivalents, your television budget swells to 135 workdays per year and 4,050 over the next 30 years. That's about 11 years worth of passivity in your future. Now that's living! Or is it?

This is not meant to suggest that leisure pursuits are worthless or that we should be busily working on something "productive" every waking moment. Far from it. As we shall see later in this chapter, it is essential to plan for and include a certain amount of rest and relaxation in even the most hectic schedules. But all aspects of our time needs must be in balance and given their proper allocation of time. The danger with television watching is that it so easily can expand to the extent it crowds out other activities we might prefer to pursue, if only we thought about it.

We have been using the term "spending" when discussing the amount of time devoted to watching television. Maybe we should say "squandering" instead. If, as a leader and manager, you truly would rather use the time you have left in your life in this manner than doing anything else, then you are fine. You need not do anything to change. But if you think you could use some of that TV time, or time now spent on any relatively unrewarding pursuit, doing something more fulfilling for you, your family, your professional life, your community, or your world. . .then you are ready to begin making some changes. Read on.

Put First Things First and Last Things Away

There are never enough hours in the day to do everything you want or need to do. Since time is a finite, scarce, non-renewable and precious resource, it must be spent where it will do the most good. The only way to do this effectively and consistently is to set priorities, something many people either fail to do at all or do in a haphazard, inconsistent way.

To be truly effective, our priority system should include all aspects of our lives: professional and personal, family and friends, occupation and avocations. To ensure that we give each area the appropriate amount of attention needed to keep our lives in balance and to keep us on track toward our long-term goals in each area, we must think through our priorities, i.e., what matters most to us. This will take some effort. We often live and work on autopilot without pausing to evaluate the ultimate worth and focus of the way we are spending our time, but unless we put some thought into such priorities, we are likely to drift aimlessly through life. We will probably wind up overemphasizing some things and short-changing or forever ignoring others, including pursuits we would consider very important if we only thought about them.

Additionally, our priority system must take into account long-term, intermediate-term, and short-term goals. Many people hope "someday" to achieve certain goals, be they material, professional, or personal, but unless these long-range aspirations are given appropriate attention in a person's daily planning, nothing will ever happen to turn these hopes into something more tangible. Dreams that are never channeled into and through a pipeline pointed toward reality will ever remain pipe dreams.

At work, some of our priorities are set for us by our bosses and high-ranking clients. Many of our tasks have deadline dates that drive their priority up. Still other duties are largely left to our own discretion. We each need a priority ranking system that we can consistently apply to demands on our time so that we can focus our time where it will be most productive to our organization, our office, and ourselves personally.

The 80/20 rule says that you will, on average, derive 80% of your benefit from 20% of your work. In business, usually 80% of the sales come from 20% of the customers. In non-profit work or personal activities, a similar principle applies, except the benefits are generally not measured in dollars but rather in client satisfaction, productivity, personal progress, etc. The key is to determine which of your clients, duties, and tasks constitute that vital 20% that will yield the greatest return so that you can focus most of your efforts where they will do the most good. It is a form of triage, made necessary by the sad fact that the demand for your time exceeds the supply. You certainly cannot leave this determination up to your clients because all of them will claim to be in the golden 20% that is deserving of your fullest attention!

Especially in the work setting, but also for personal priorities, many successful people assign a number or a letter to each task, such as 1, 2, 3 or A, B, C, to categorize them into urgent, routine, and maybe-mañana levels of significance. Others have three stacks on their desk, or three large folders, that can serve the same function. The particular method you choose is not nearly as important as choosing a method you will actually use. Pick one that fits your personal style, and stick with it. This will take some discipline, but you can do it!

Do not allow your priority system to be taken prisoner, and your life thereby controlled by tasks that are urgent but not important. Some things are very significant to us, whether on a professional or personal basis, yet are not urgent. They do not have to be done by a specific, near-term date and time, yet if we leave them undone, there will eventually be serious consequences. A prime example is physical exercise. It is rarely if ever crucial that we work out at a particular point in time, but if we allow exercise to be subordinated to more "urgent" matters continually, at some point our health will suffer, we will be less productive, and we will lose much more time (and even our lives) than if we had regularly disciplined ourselves to do it.

Personal and professional development, including learning new skills, keeping current, networking, and other maintenance and improvement activities, are not urgent in the sense that they must be done by noon today but are, nonetheless, very important. Be sure to budget time for them accordingly, and do not let them be parasitized by seemingly hot but ultimately less significant activities. A ringing telephone, a co-worker with his hair (figuratively) on fire, a "priority" e-mail message—these are very hard to ignore or to put on the back burner, but, many times, that is exactly what should be done. It is the underlying significance of the message, not the frantic manner in which it cries out for your attention, that should determine priority.

Imagine the various demands on your time as a baby. A baby will cry and scream for many reasons. Some of those reasons, such as physical pain or illness, genuinely call for immediate attention. Others are important in the mind of the infant but can probably wait a while without any truly adverse consequences if you are otherwise occupied. Do not let your schedule be hijacked by the office equivalent of a squalling baby who wants her brown teddy bear instead of her pink one.

Top priority items, whatever their level of urgency, do not necessarily always get worked first. You may find it more efficient to knock off a quick but lower priority item during a short block of time first thing in the morning and then get to higher priority items a little later when more time is available or when other people are around to help you. The most important thing is to know the priority of each item and plan your day or week to give each item the time it needs.

Better Left Undone?

If it is not worth doing at all, do not do it. Certain tasks are meaningless and wasteful and should not take up anyone's time. Use the Quality system to identify these and, with proper coordination through the organization's decision-making system, eliminate them. Ask the hard questions: What is the value added from this task? If I—or we—give this project maximum effort and develop it to its fullest potential, what will be the benefit? If it is not worth the time and effort, it is essentially a parasite and doing it would rob scarce resources from more important actions. Just because something has been done for a long time and has acquired a life of its own does not mean it is worthwhile.

Unproductive work tends to breed more unproductive work. You need meetings, reports, files, Process Action Teams, metrics, and other administrivia to monitor and support it. Worst of all, doing unproductive work can delude you into thinking you are doing something useful when, in fact, you are not. Since time is finite and scarce, these tasks parasitize other, more useful projects.

Meetings can be a prime example of unproductive time. Unless meetings have a definable, verifiable purpose, and a realistic prospect of yielding more benefits than the resources they consume, they should not be held. Some otherwise useful meetings are held more frequently than needed. And every meeting should have an agenda with specific topics and objectives, within a definite concluding time. Use the Quality process to trim the fat from necessary meetings and to abolish unnecessary meetings. If you succeed in doing so, your grateful and astonished co-workers will probably put up a twenty-five-foot-tall bronze statue of you, in heroic pose and classical garb, in front of the building.

In our personal lives as well, some activities probably should be dropped in favor of others. With so little time available to devote to all phases of life, something has to give. Let it be something we can afford to give up rather than something we will later deeply regret not doing. If it is a choice between watching one more hour of TV each day and spending an hour reading aloud with our families, which one better fits into our priority planning? Would we rather devote thirty minutes each week to playing computer games or talking on the telephone with our friends and relatives? Do we spend as much time reading as we would like to, and is the type of material we read consistent with our goals? Is so-called "quality time" with our children adequate, or could something be gained by beefing up the quantity of time we spend with them if we perhaps cut back on menial tasks? Each person must ask, and answer, these and many other similar questions for himself or herself. The answers will vary from person to person and may even change over time. But we will never know unless we ask.

This process of evaluating the importance of each thing we do can be frightening. What if it turns out that nothing we do at work really means much to anybody? What if our leisure pursuits are taking too much time from things we would really like to accomplish with our lives and making it impossible for us to achieve them? What if the Emperor has no clothes?

Hard questions sometimes do lead to hard, unpleasant answers. But is it not better to discover the truth before it is too late to do anything about it? If we want to be able someday to look back on the way we spent our lives and view the results with justifiable pride and a sense of fulfillment, we need to make sure we are living and working accordingly. If we are not, we need to change, as did Ebenezer Scrooge in Dickens' "A Christmas Carol." No matter how old we are, and regardless of how deeply entrenched we are in our personal habits, as long as we are alive, there is still the opportunity for positive change. We need to find within ourselves the courage and resolve to make that change. That is what true leaders do, after all.

Lists: Much "To-do" About Everything

Write down the things you need to do. Once you write something down, your subconscious mind is free to work on problem solving rather than remembering. It can be nerve-wracking as well as inefficient and dangerous to try to keep our "to-do" information in our heads. But writing each item down, somewhere, anywhere, is only the beginning and is not an end in itself.

Have at least one consolidated place where all your "to-do" tasks will be listed. Do not rely on lots of post-its and scattered notes. If you use one list, it will be easier to focus on your priority items and harder to forget anything. Many people make the mistake of having their daily activities, meetings, appointments, and projects memorialized in a bewildering array of different forms. Some things are written down in an appointment book where they then co-exist along with random phone numbers, addresses, ideas, laundry tickets, and cereal coupons. Some tasks are jotted down on post-its that proliferate until they obscure the entire surface of desks, computer screens, walls, refrigerators, and bulletin boards like nuclear fallout after a blast. Some notes are scribbled on a multitude of scraps of paper that pile up until they tower over us, both literally and figuratively, as a veritable "Mount To-do," and defy us to scale them. Some items are entered into a computerized scheduler and then hardly ever checked again. Some are written on what was originally intended to be a complete list but has never matured to that level.

This cannot work for long. It creates the danger that whoever needs the information will fail to look at all the various places that must be checked to be sure nothing important is hiding anywhere. There are just too many good hiding places in such a system and vital tasks and appointments can go underground for an extended period. There must be one master list, and that one list must be used exclusive of all other options. Tell yourself that if you do not put something in your master list, you are effectively deciding not to do it. Make this one list the only possible habitat where the species known as "To-dos" has any hope of survival; your "to-dos" must be placed in this sanctuary, or they will die.

As a fail-safe, you might consider having a back-up list, either in hard copy or on computer, but this is only to be used in case something horrible happens to the master list. You must not leave any room for doubt. There can be no other place where "to-dos" might be allowed to roost. The rule is simple, and it even rhymes: If it's not on the list, it just doesn't exist.

Check your master list frequently and regularly at specific times, such as at the beginning, middle, and ending of every day. This will keep you on course and show you where you need to focus your energies. You may want to keep your list on top of your desk or taped to the wall next to it so it is in constant view. You can cross off or check off items as you complete them, and the sight of such progress in front of your eyes may inspire you to further triumphs!

Include both short-term and long-term projects on your master list. This will prevent deadlines and important but far-off tasks from sneaking up on you. Long-term items must be included and perhaps subdivided into more short-term sub-projects. This is an excellent way to get moving and then monitor progress toward your goals, which so easily can get lost in the blizzard of day-to-day business and craziness.

One very important type of list is the checklist. Checklists can be highly efficient tools for organizing your efforts. Some may already be available for certain tasks in your office, such as the processing of frequently recurring types of paperwork. You may be able to use these with minor adjustments for your unique situation. For other recurring functions, you may need to develop your own checklist, complete with time standards for meeting certain milestones. The proper use of checklists is an excellent way to avoid forgetting key points and to stay on schedule.

Files Yes, Piles No

For many people, their natural habitat seems to be the chaos theory come to life. Every square inch of floors, desks, tables, counter tops, dressers—any relatively flat surface—tends to be covered with a miniature mountain range of more-or-less vertical piles of varying heights, including Mount To-do and many others. These tiny Himalayas are made, not of stone, but of newspapers, magazines, documents, mail, and assorted other debris. No less than Mount Everest, such slopes pose a staggering challenge to the human spirit!

Who can hope to scale such peaks? How can anyone locate anything amidst all the rubble? Who could reach the summit without the aid of supplemental oxygen? The best way, it turns out, is to level the mountains and start over.

When you have a project to work on, create a folder for it and it alone. Give the folder a prominent and appropriately descriptive label so you will know what it is supposed to be about. Put all the folders in one place, maybe even–shocking as it might seem–a file cabinet, in alphabetical order. Leave nothing out. Either it is important enough to deserve a decent home in a respectable folder, or it should be thrown out.

This will be difficult and perhaps deeply disturbing for those whose credo is "Pile, don't file." But be strong. Join a support group if you must, but wade right in and tackle the mountains you have created. It will get easier once you become accustomed to more level terrain.

From now on, as you get ideas or gather material for each project, put it in the appropriate folder and leave it there until you need it again. When you take something out of the folder to use it, be sure to put it right back in its home again immediately after you have stopped using it. For large, complex projects, you may need subdivisions within the main folder to make it easier to stay organized; the concept is identical in any event. Do not write unrelated matters on the same sheet of paper or card; you cannot stay organized if you let extraneous materials elbow their way into the home you have provided for your project. If you open the door to such intruders, they will soon claim squatter's rights and you will have a hard time weeding them out, attached as they are to proper residents of the folder.

You will be amazed by the difference this magnificent new high-tech invention, the file folder, can make. After a while, you will begin to glimpse bare spots on your floors, and eventually even on your desk. And whenever you need to retrieve a document, you will no longer have to form a search party and launch a three-day rescue expedition, complete with helicopter support. You will actually be able to locate a folder that contains your document, without delay and panic. And you will find that it is taking you less time to get more work done.

You Are Not Paid by the Word

One primary enemy of effective time management is word inflation. Every word that is spoken or written or typed takes time away from at least one person—the person who said or wrote or typed it. Potentially, every word also takes time from the receiver, as well, who must listen to or read it. In this era of mass communication, with e-mail and websites, there can be multitudes of receivers for each word that is transmitted via these means. Seen in this light, words have a great potential to waste time if they are not used judiciously.

Try to be succinct. Anyone who can write plainly and concisely is a national treasure. If you have succeeded in making your paper mountains flat, you are ready for this challenge too. Brevity can save you a great deal of time.

This is virtually contrary to the natural order of the universe for some people. Particularly within certain professions, such as the law and politics, people often speak and write as if they were paid by the word. Why use two words when two dozen will do?

Yet more is not more in this context, both for purposes of time management and in terms of the effectiveness of the communication. Short, simple, punchy messages are more likely to be read or listened to, and more likely to be remembered, than long-winded gabfests. Professional advertisers know this, and we all can learn something valuable from their examples. If you do not put your audience to sleep, you have a better chance of persuading them.

This economy of words is effective for our own internal uses just as it is for our communications with others. Use abbreviations and acronyms wherever possible as you take notes or jot down ideas, assignments, directions, etc. Be consistent so co-workers (especially any administrative assistants you might have) can decipher your code; make a list of your commonly used abbreviations for them.

Use the computer to create and modify sample letters for your recurring tasks. A well-crafted shell can be used for a host of repetitive tasks. Then you can customize them to fit the particular facts and circumstances of each specific project. Also, you can cut and paste, electronically speaking, entire sections of frequently used text without the need to recreate it every time. This is a tremendous time-saver for people who deal with documents that are only partially modified from case to case.

Hunting for Buried Treasure Time

Do you ever find yourself a captive audience of one with nothing happening on stage? Are you ever frustrated because you are trapped in a situation where you have nothing to do but wait? Does your life sometimes feel like one giant waiting area at the Department of Motor Vehicles? If not, congratulations; chances are you are a fictional hero from a thrilling novel rather than a real person living in today's real world.

Modern life is full of "hurry up and wait" situations. We get stuck in traffic. We are kept waiting at the doctor's and dentist's office. People schedule meetings and other events and then fail to begin them on time. The effect can be maddening and wasteful. But to paraphrase the famous line from the film *Animal House* " don't get mad–get busy."

We all have downtime that we could use in more productive ways than just grumbling about how lousy the situation may be. Bring something worthwhile to read when there is any chance you will be kept waiting, e.g., the clinic, the boss's office, airports, at traffic lights, the conference room, the theater, sporting events, on planes, on buses and subway trains. Every little bit helps. You could bring a tape recorder, electronic note-taker, or a pad of paper, too, and put some thoughts down for future use. Car phones or other mobile phones are useful, too, if employed wisely.

In addition to time spent waiting for events to begin, some events present opportunities for finding time treasure within the events themselves. For example, most sporting events have considerable amounts of downtime that could be used. Much of this time comes between quarters, innings, halves, or periods. There is also a lot of time between plays in football and between pitches in baseball as well as occasions when there is a time-out for reasons of injury, player changes, etc. You can steal back sizable amounts of time, in little bite-size chunks, by reading or writing during these breaks in the action.

These snippets of time treasure are useful for some productive activities, but many projects are much more effectively accomplished where you can focus on them for longer periods. For such projects, try to create relatively long blocks of time that you can devote exclusively to certain tasks without interruption and give yourself a chance to enter the "flow" state where you are particularly productive and creative. Interruptions break your concentration and force you to stop and start over repeatedly thereby losing momentum and mental focus. There are several ways to arrange for uninterrupted time blocks.

By arriving earlier or leaving later than most others, you can often get a large amount of work done without phone interruptions or people dropping in on you. In addition, during the heart of the day it may be possible to arrange for your phone calls to be held (perhaps with some key exceptions) for a certain period. Try to schedule meetings so that they do not unnecessarily carve up your day. Even away from the office, you can make this principle work for you; business trips can be a good source of uninterrupted time away from the phone and the usual office visitors.

We have mentioned time consumed by being stuck in traffic. Commuting, whether by car, bus, or train, takes a sizable chunk out of many daily schedules. Fight back! There are some things you can do. For example, drive to and from work earlier or later than the masses to avoid traffic jams. It may even be possible to avoid commuting all together, at least on certain days. Could you work at home and "telecommute?" Every time you do, you save all the time you would have lost to the daily trek to and from work. Alternative work schedules, which often provide for longer hours on some days in exchange for an extra day off every two weeks or so, can also help, as long as the longer days do not cause you to spend much more time in traffic or overtax your stamina.

In your personal life, the same precepts apply. Try to live "off peak," i.e., to do things when most other people are not doing them, so you will not be kept waiting any more than necessary. In addition to trying to avoid commuting to and from work during rush hour, also avoid leisure travel during the times of heaviest traffic. Do not cash checks or buy groceries on pay day when the banks and supermarkets are clogged with long lines of people crowding their way, inch by inch, to the head of the line. Avoid going to the post office on or just before the annual "Tax Day" of April 15 or shortly before Christmas. Buy holiday gifts at any time other than the weeks just before the end of the year. When you dine out at a heavily-patronized restaurant, either make a reservation in advance or go before the evening rush; you may even qualify for early-bird special prices. The same is true for attending popular films. Make appointments to get your hair cut rather than just walking in and waiting for your turn. These may seem like little things, and some of them are, but over the span of weeks, months, and years, they can add up to significant savings of time and money.

The First Step Is a Lulu

Do not waste time commencing to proceed to get ready to get started. Procrastinators are always almost on the verge of toying with the notion of thinking of getting the job done. Often, beginning is half the job. The clean sheet of paper or the blank computer screen is a formidable barrier to accomplishment. Once you take the first few steps, even small ones, it is much easier to follow through to completion because then momentum is on your side and inertia is overcome. As Sir Isaac Newton observed, objects at rest tend to stay at rest, and objects in motion tend to stay in motion. The same goes double for people. Particularly with difficult or unpleasant tasks that you might be dreading and worrying about, it is best to tackle them early and get them over with.

If you need to prepare an after-action report on an event or to file a travel voucher, the best time is now. Your memory is at its freshest, and the necessary documents are at your fingertips. If you delay, you will find a simple task becoming much more difficult. On top of your ever-fading memory and disappearing documentation, your work is made more vexing by the pressure you bring upon yourself. A looming deadline, or (horrors) a deadline that has already passed you by, can inflict needless tension and stress upon you. And you don't really have a shortage of either one, do you?

It may seem strange, but even typing the subject line on a document can have a very real and beneficial effect on the brand of writer's block we are discussing. The simple act of getting started–of opening a new word processing document and saving it with a descriptive name or scrawling a title on a previously and oppressively blank sheet of paper–can open the floodgates. You are no longer stuck in that horrid wasteland of "Not Even Started." Psychologically, the smallest of first steps can significantly release pre-project tension and release your pent-up capabilities. Put something, anything, on paper. The remainder will follow more easily as a result.

An issue that requires research can be difficult because it is hard to know when you have done enough groundwork and can safely commence writing the report. But it is critical to develop the decisiveness necessary to "freeze the design" as the engineers say, at some reasonable point, and get on with it. If you have left some important stone unturned, this will usually become apparent as you write your report or memorandum. If you do not know exactly how the story ends when you begin writing it, you will probably find out by the time you need to know just because that act of writing will force you to consider all of the issues within one logical framework.

Wanted, for Grand Theft Chrono: Time Thieves

No one enjoys having his or her valuables stolen. We take significant precautions to prevent people from stealing our wallets, our cars, and our household valuables. If we catch someone attempting to commit such acts of larceny, we stop them and take steps to prevent any further similar crimes. Yet, many of us are amazingly tolerant of time thieves.

People who waste your time are time thieves. They steal something from you more valuable than money, something that can never be replaced. Learn who these time thieves are and develop methods for avoiding them.

One common technique of time thieves is chronic tardiness of the type that makes others wait for them. Do you really want to continue allowing these people to make your schedule subservient to theirs or to their lack of a schedule? You cannot allow time thieves to pick your pocket; you must take action. If, for example, people routinely are late for appointments with you and they are not in a position of authority over you, consider countermeasures such as not seeing them unless they are on time, praising them when they are, having a heart-to-heart chat with them, or cutting back on your associations with them. You can also try scheduling very specific appointments at odd times, such as 4:05, and emphasize when making the arrangements that you need to meet right at that time because you have other appointments pending.

If your time thieves are also your superiors, this is obviously a more delicate situation, but there are still techniques you can use without ending your career. If they are in another office, try to befriend their secretary or executive assistant (their "gatekeeper"). Such a person can feed you inside information as to whether and by how much their boss is running late, and, thereby, save you waiting time. You can also bring something with you to do while you wait, as discussed earlier.

If your time thief is your spouse or significant other, this last approach is probably your best bet, assuming you would like to continue in your relationship. Or, you might lovingly suggest that he or she would enjoy reading this delightful chapter in this most fascinating book. Maybe such subtle missionary work will win a convert to the cause of effective time management and in the process win you a reformed and former time thief.

Some time thieves operate by getting you to do their work for them. Co-workers and even subordinates sometimes cleverly involve us in what should be their responsibility, taking advantage of our wish to be helpful and our genial good nature. Helpfulness is a wonderful trait, but make sure you stop short of doing other people's work. Some of us are too good for our own good. And, of course, if we continually do someone else's work, we deprive that person of the opportunity to learn and grow and gain experience. Any parent of school-age children knows the fallacy of "helping" a child by doing that child's homework for him or her. In the long run, we do people no great favor by repeatedly bailing them out in this manner. We lose time, and they lose the chance to become more capable, more competent, and more independent.

Other time thieves come disguised in a friendly and talkative camouflage. Such people seem to occupy themselves for much of the workday by strolling from office to office, chatting about events and opinions great and small. Charming and congenial, they love to engage their co-workers in stimulating conversation concerning everything from yesterday's sporting events to global political crises. "Did you see that game?" "Can you believe what's happening in Washington DC?" It is so easy to get pulled into these live talk-shows, but once you are in, it is not so easy to get out. The "hosts" of these miniature talk shows are essentially Oprah in your office, but you cannot change the channel or shut off the TV. Or can you?

We are not suggesting that you be unfriendly or turn into a hermit who hides behind a closed and locked office door all day, every day. Some amount of socializing is rewarding and good, both because it is enjoyable and because it can facilitate more effective interactions with other people. As always, the key is to know how much is enough and to keep things in balance.

Develop time cues, both oral and physical, both to schedule a meeting and to terminate one. If a specific time is important to you, say so clearly and give a reason such as "We need to meet (or break this off) at 4:30 and not a minute later, because I have to meet with someone else at 4:45." If you are more flexible, say "I will meet you at 4:30-ish or thereabouts." When calling to confirm an appointment, tell the gatekeeper, "I am on a very tight schedule today, so I wanted to check if 3:05 still looks like a realistic time for me to see Ms. Lee." When calling someone, announce up front, "Do you have two minutes for just a couple of quick questions?" When you receive a call at a bad time say, "You caught me right in between meetings, so unfortunately, I only have five minutes. I really want to talk to you, so should we schedule another time when we will not have to rush?" When nearing the point at which you want to end a phone conversation or an informal in-person chat, say "Joe, before I have to leave for my next appointment, I have one thing to ask you," or "Before we stop, I need to tell you one thing."

Physical cues include leaning forward in your chair, gathering papers in preparation for leaving, beginning to look for items on your desk, or even standing up. In conversation, pause longer and longer between your remarks and say the bare minimum when you do speak. You can provide less eye contact and less non-verbal affirmation of what the other person is saying. If all else fails and, based on your experiences with a particular time thief, you anticipate trouble ending the meeting, you can arrange in advance for one of your office personnel to interrupt after a certain amount of time or upon some signal from you to remind you of another commitment. The cavalry to the rescue! You need not and usually should not be impolite, but you do need to keep even the most pleasant time thieves from robbing you blind.

Don't Hesitate to Delegate

As a leader, if somebody else within your span of control in the organization can do a task quicker, better, or cheaper than you can, delegate it to them whenever possible. Although administrative support personnel are a scarce commodity, try to use them to the maximum feasible extent for things like photocopying, typing, faxing, filing, and other clerical functions. Focus on the work you are specifically tasked to do, and wherever possible do only what only you can do. You are the leader. You are paid to lead, not to do all the groundwork. If you get too tangled in the thicket of non-leader work, you may never find your way out again. Delegate before it is too late!

This is very difficult for some leaders to do because they fear that no one else can get things done as well as they can, and they do not want to lose control. But such leaders pay a heavy price for their failure to delegate. They work far too many hours, while people who are paid to help them go home early. Moreover, they cannot be fully functional as leaders because too much of their energy and time is expended on tasks that do not contribute to their primary purpose. What is wrong with this picture? Plenty.

Our subordinates are often capable of much more than we think they are. Unless we give them proper training and experience, in part by delegating, they will not develop their full potential or reach their peak value to our office. Many people would appreciate a chance to do more challenging work and learn new skills. Of course, training, mentoring, and supervision take time, but the benefits will very often be worth it. As described in our chapter on mentoring, it is particularly important to learn what our subordinates' professional goals are and then help them to achieve those goals. What we delegate to them can be geared toward their interests and aspirations.

Effective delegation requires that the delegatee fully understand the instructions (including the deadline), feel the assignment is important, know what tools and resources are available to assist in completing the work, have some method of progress reporting and accountability, know the consequences of both a good and a bad job, and understand why the work needs to be done. You should keep a record of what you delegate, complete with the deadline date, so you can monitor the progress of the work (perhaps by requiring periodic reports from the delegatee) and retain ultimate control over it.

Never downplay the significance of any task you delegate by referring to it as a "no-brainer" or "light work"; if the delegatee does not believe it is of value, why should he or she devote any effort to it? Delegation is a form of teaching, and a crucial part of that process is to teach people what we do and why we do it.

Until you are confident in your subordinates' ability to handle the work, begin by delegating simpler, less critical projects. Be very explicit in your instructions, especially at first. Get the delegatee to explain the project to you in his or her own words, so you can be assured that everyone involved comprehends what has to be done. Then, check the progress periodically, so you can make any necessary adjustments in what the delegatee is doing before it is too late. If the delegatee performs successfully, you can gradually and incrementally move to more complex, risky work. At each stage, ensure you prepare your people properly and provide adequate training and resources to do the job.

Give credit where credit is due. If a delegatee's efforts contributed to a successful product, tell him or her so. More importantly, tell your supervisor, and be generous with your praise, especially in public. Say "thank you" at every opportunity. Thank you notes and letters of appreciation are important tools of the trade. Help people to feel good about themselves and about their work, and they will help you in return.

The delegation principle applies at home as well as at work. Unless money is very tight, or you truly enjoy such activities, hire someone else to do your yardwork, home repair, vehicle maintenance, major housekeeping, and other time consuming jobs. Maybe you can even get by with less total effort in these areas. Your time is too valuable to devote to unpleasant or menial labor unless absolutely necessary. Only do it yourself if you genuinely would prefer to keep the money and lose the time. Remember, free time is not free; it is very valuable!

We are not advocating that you let your yard go unmown until it qualifies for wilderness designation or that you vacuum your carpets only once per Olympiad or that you let the oil remain in your car until it is old enough to vote. A certain amount of tending, cleaning, and maintaining is essential for quality of life and peaceful coexistence with one's neighbors and significant others. But some people spend too much time on these activities, so much so that they rarely, if ever, have any time left over to work on projects with a greater long-term payoff. Maybe by settling for a small reduction in these frequently recurring activities we can find more time for those oft-neglected things we are always meaning to "get around to someday."

Do It Right the First Time

Carpenters have a maxim, "Measure twice, cut once." This principle, as well as the more widely known cliché "haste makes waste," applies directly to time management. Too many people, in trying to hurry, make errors that necessitate redoing the project and in the final analysis taking much more time. It is far preferable to spend a little extra time initially to double-check your ground rules, ensure you are doing what needs to be done, and verify that what you have done is accurate and complete before you send it on down the line. If you take these precautions at the outset, you can rest assured that you will probably never have to re-visit that project.

One obvious but often neglected aspect of doing it right the first time is to check your spelling carefully. Always use the spell-checker on your computer, but please, please, do not stop there. Computer spell-checkers will miss many errors, causing you much embarrassment and more work. Remember this poem:

> I have a spelling checker.
> It came with my PC.
> It plainly marks four my revue,
> Mistakes I cannot sea.
> I've run this poem threw it,
> I'm sure your please too no.
> Its letter perfect in it's weigh,
> My checker tolled me sew.

Use spell-checkers as a supplement to, not a replacement for, your own meticulous, personal, proofreading efforts. If possible, have a colleague proofread your work too, and do the same for them in return. If you use this two-proofreader method, start at opposite ends of the material; people sometimes get tired and careless while proofing, especially when a lengthy and complex document is involved. Reading the text aloud can also catch errors that may be easily skimmed over when reading silently.

A partner in accuracy can be a very valuable asset. In addition to catching spelling errors, a second brain can lend useful insight into technical analysis, logical reasoning, factual errors, unclear communication, and other areas. Take the small amount of extra time up front to run your work past your partner first, and you may save yourself ten times that amount in revisions and rewrites later.

Planning can be another big time saver. The investment in time spent on planning usually is recouped with interest. Before you plunge into a project, think through each step, jotting down what you need to do, what resources you will need to help you, and when you will need them. You do not want to find yourself, three weeks into a project, unable to proceed any further until you obtain something that will take two weeks to arrive or until the person you must meet with returns from an extended leave of absence. Think things through first, including what you will need from other people and other sources.

If you are running a meeting, prepare and distribute an agenda to all attendees at least a day in advance; include background materials as attachments, along with a clearly defined purpose for the meeting and specifically what you want it to accomplish. This will help all attendees to come prepared and make the meeting more efficient and productive. If people at the meeting are equipped with everything they need, you might actually get something done at the meeting rather than deferring it until later.

Organization is closely related to planning. If you know where everything belongs, and make sure it goes there, you will not have to waste time searching for it. As we mentioned earlier, your filing system should make sense and be user friendly. Once you have a workable system, use it religiously. If you do not need to form a posse every time you want to locate a document, you will have more time for other things.

This applies to physical items too, both at home and at work. Do you regularly have to drop everything and bloodhound your way to whatever new hiding place is concealing your car keys, your eyeglasses, your wallet, your cell phone, your checkbook, your unpaid bills, your income tax documents, or your shopping list? Come on, now; we know who you are. Admit it! That is the first step toward recovery.

Your grandmother may have told you, "A place for everything and everything in its place." She was right. If you can manage to establish one and only one logical, reasonably accessible and convenient place where you always, without fail, keep each one of these things, you will be well on your way to a less chaotic life. As with a filing system, it will be strange and difficult at first, but if you can stay with it, you will eventually form a very good habit.

Are your children or pets partially responsible for making your home a giant three-dimensional version of "Where's Waldo?" If so, try to select the "place for everything" so as to be relatively safe from these helpful assistants who would move your items to where they want them. Given the chance, your little helpers will reorganize your home so extensively that it will look as if you were recently moved in by the "Two Babies and a Truck" moving company. You may run out of high-altitude or locked places for your key items, but until you do, choose them and use them. You will spend less time running around in frantic search for lost articles and have more time available for other frantic pursuits.

Phone Techniques

Should time-conscious people build a shrine to Alexander Graham Bell or vote him into the Hall of Shame? The answer depends on each individual. The telephone can be an effective time saver, if used properly.

Unfortunately, many people let the phone be a drain on their time rather than an efficient tool. This Jekyll and Hyde phenomenon makes wise use of the telephone an especially important aspect of any time management effort.

As with anything else, preparation is the key. If you do not think about your phone use in advance, with an eye toward making it work for you rather than vice versa, nothing will change.

It is helpful to prepare a script or at least an outline before an important or complex call. It will ensure you cover everything you need to, help you to stay organized, and guard against long, rambling conversations. If you have something particularly complex or emotionally delicate to say, having it scripted out in advance can help you avoid potential trouble with word choice as well.

Minimize the amount of time you spend telling your story to people who cannot help you. Briefly explain the nature of your call and get transferred to the right person as soon as possible. Executive assistants and high-level secretaries are usually knowledgeable about who handles what in their organizations. Once you get through to the right person, try to get his or her direct phone number; then you will not have to go through the gatekeeper again.

Make a note of the name and direct extension of every person to whom you speak, especially the gatekeepers for important points of contact. You will be able to find them again if need be, and you will make them feel better if you use their names as you speak to them.

If you regularly must call an office with a lengthy automated recitation of options ("If your hair is currently on fire, press One now."), try to cut down on the amount of time you spend listening to this incantation. Write down the numbers of the options you usually use so you can enter them at the outset. Do the same for the direct extension of the persons you usually deal with. Life is too short to spend listening to a robot tell you which button to push next.

When you do get to speak with an actual person in real time, always identify yourself, by name and organization, in the first sentence you speak. It is courteous, and it saves the other party from having to ask you these routine questions.

To minimize your telephone tag playing time, if your party is in a meeting or on another call, ask whether a note can be slipped to them indicating you can hold if they will be available shortly. If they are too busy, ask whether you can make an appointment to call them back at a specific time. If you are given such an appointment, be sure to call back at precisely that time.

If you are trying to reach a high-ranking person, try calling very early in the morning or after normal business hours. At such times, they are more likely to be in the office rather than in meetings or other out-of-office activities. Also, their gatekeepers are less likely to be present to screen you out; the boss may even be answering the phones personally. Moreover, a side benefit is that you may impress them by appearing to be working at an hour when others are not, a technique made famous by the character J. Pierpont Finch in the musical play *How to Succeed in Business Without Really Trying.*

Conference calls, including video teleconferencing, can save enormous amounts of time. Entire business trips can be obviated by a well-planned conference call involving all the key players. At a minimum, they save you the time of calling each person individually and then back-briefing the rest of them as to what each one says. Try using these electronic meetings in lieu of the more traditional in-person meetings. Even if it saves people from going across town, let alone across the country, it will be worthwhile. Although there will always be great value in making and renewing in-person connections, electronic meetings can safely be used at least part of the time.

Let us say a few words about the great modern sport of telephone tag, which threatens to displace baseball as the "National Pastime." If someone calls and leaves a message for you, return the call immediately. It is the polite thing to do, and you are more likely to catch the person at his or her desk than if you wait until later. Memories will be fresh, relevant documents will be handy, and you can get things done quickly and efficiently. Your callers will appreciate your prompt replies, too, because so few people make the effort to return calls in a timely manner.

Instruct the persons who answer your office phones to slip you a note if someone else calls while you are on the phone or speaking with someone in person. You can then let them know whether you will take the new call immediately or in one minute or will have to return the call shortly. Also, leave messages for the people you call that they should have you interrupted if you are otherwise occupied when they call you back. This will make them understand that their call is important to you. This will also reduce telephone tag and allow you to inject some sense of priorities into your phone calls. You do not want the CEO to be told you are on the phone and unavailable when you are simply calling the local movie theater to listen to their recorded message of what is playing!

If you are having a lot of trouble reaching someone on the phone or you cannot find another way to end your marathon game of telephone tag, send a fax. It will generally get to the person quickly and be read without much delay. At least your side of the message will get through. E-mail can also be an alternative, although it depends on the recipient actually checking and reading his or her e-mail messages promptly. Many do, but there are still some people who routinely ignore their e-mail for extended periods. If you use the e-mail option, first do your homework and learn how often the other person partakes of his or her electron-laden postings.

If you do not have an answering machine or voice mail system, get one and use it. If the person you call has an answering machine or voice mail, leave a very detailed message, not just that you called. Few things are as irritating as people who call and leave messages saying nothing more than that they called or, even worse, the folks who refuse to "talk to a machine" at all and summarily hang up. What are they afraid of? Do they think an evil creature from outer space will snake through the phone lines and invade their brains like something from the "Aliens" movies if they leave a message on your machine?

When you get an answering machine or voice mail instead of reaching your person "live," consider it just as good as if you had struck pay dirt. Why not tell them what you wanted to tell them? You can often get your entire message across, on tape, and without having to be filtered through the administrative assistant's brain, if you clearly and succinctly tell it to the machine. Sometimes, even if a secretary answers, you can ask to leave your message on voice mail. This eliminates many errors that otherwise might creep into your message because you can tell your story directly, in your own words, in the level of detail you want, and with your own vocal inflection. Your party can even listen to your message multiple times, if necessary, and make sure there is no misunderstanding. This is an advantage not present when you are actually conversing with someone in real time, akin to having a verbatim record of the entire communication. So, do not be a wimp when it comes to leaving recorded messages; they are useful tools, and you can make them work for you.

Use Computers, Don't Let Them Use You

Please do not fall into the trap of assuming, as a leader and manager, that you need not know anything about computers. The days when that was true expired along with the disco craze, streaking, and mood rings. If you are not computer literate, or if computers scare you, now would be an excellent time to break down those barriers and use that big hunk of metal and plastic sitting in your office as more than an expensive display board for post-it notes. Computers can help you make a quantum leap forward in your productivity, efficiency, and effectiveness. . .if you will let them.

We have already noted the timesaving benefits of word processors. In addition to quick and easy corrections and editing, they allow us to use sample documents, or templates, for frequently recurring products, as well as canned chunks of often-used text for cutting and pasting wherever needed. Keep a library of such useful word processing documents on disks, including memos and reports that are likely to be useful in the future. There is no need to begin again from scratch when a little foresight can give you a big head start.

Computer-aided research can be a lifesaver. With a little practice, you can become adept at crafting search requests and be both faster and more thorough than you could ever be with the books. And with our hard-copy libraries withering away, computer-aided research will soon be a necessity, not a luxury.

Worldwide web sites exist in astonishing numbers and for virtually every subject imaginable. You may be accustomed to taking the time to travel to a conventional library, manually looking up potential resources in the card catalogue, physically locating books that might be on point, poring through each volume to ascertain whether it can be helpful, and either photocopying applicable portions or taking notes on the sections you need. While familiar and somewhat pleasant, this traditional means of finding and accessing information is much slower and inefficient than even marginally competent web research.

With the aid of a computer, a modem, and knowledge of a few simple techniques, any literate person can, in effect, gain the benefits of a complete and lengthy trip to a vast library within minutes and without ever leaving the room. A little experimentation and experience will quickly bring most people to the stage where they can choose appropriate key words and search terms and zero in on the most likely sources of information among the myriad possibilities the computer will discover. It is well worth the time it takes to acquire these skills, and, as a bonus, the process of learning about the worldwide web is actually fun.

Similarly, electronic mail is a wonderful alternative to traditional correspondence. Virtually instantaneously, entire documents, with attachments, can be sent to people in other offices and even in other cities or nations. You do not have to worry that the letter will get lost or bogged down in the U.S. Mail (now often referred to derisively as "snail mail" because of its plodding slowness when compared to e-mail) or the office distribution system. And with e-mail, often you can get immediate confirmation of receipt and a reply from the other person. If need be, you can send the same message to many different addressees all at once. As with web research, e-mail is even fun to use, and you do not need stamps. Remember, though, to find out in advance whether your intended recipient frequently checks his or her e-mail, or you might find your messages languishing unread for a long time.

To the extent you already use computers for some purposes, chances are you are barely scratching the surface of the potential benefits you might derive from the software you have. Invest some time in learning more about the capabilities of the software available to you. Tutorials, the experts at the local computer shop, short courses, printed documentation, special how-to books, the "Help" function in the software itself, and toll-free customer assistance numbers are rich sources of information. You may be amazed by some of the things your software can do for you if only you go to the trouble of discovering them.

If you need to do some of your own typing and your typing skills are not good, consider taking a course. There are also software packages that will help you learn to type or improve the skills you already have. The time you save by moving beyond the hunt-and-peck method for the rest of your life will more than justify the short period of time spent learning.

Finally, do some exploring, whether on-line or in person, and see what else exists in the world of software. There may be several software products available that would make your life easier and more enjoyable. Browse through any large software store and see what some of the products can do. Think about whether any of them would be useful to you. Do this at least every three months or so because advancements are coming at a dizzying pace. Plus–you guessed it–it is fun!

It's a Wonderful Life

It is easy to get so caught up in the time management techniques discussed in this chapter that you forget to apply them in all aspects of your life, not just at work. It is critically important not to short-change yourself in your efforts to succeed professionally. Make time for your personal interests, including friends and family. Exercise regularly. And never be too busy in the daily routine to learn new skills or update your professional knowledge.

Virtually no one on his or her deathbed regrets not spending more time at the office. People do regret not spending more time with their loved ones, or helping people, or seeing the world, or engaging in the other pursuits that make life worth living. All of these activities take time, and unless you plan for them, life will speed past you and leave you behind.

You have probably seen the famous Frank Capra film, *It's a Wonderful Life.* Recall that George Bailey, as played by Jimmy Stewart, came to a crisis point at which he wondered whether it would have been better if he had never been born. Through the intervention of an angel, he is made to see how very different the world would have been, for his family, friends, and community, if he had never existed. The experience profoundly moved him as he realized that, for all his many troubles and frustrated dreams, he really had enjoyed a wonderful life and had touched people far beyond his wildest imagination. With this new perspective, he decided he wanted very much to live again and became acutely grateful for even the most mundane facets of daily life. . .even those, such as the loose knob on his creaky stairway banister, that he had previously found annoying.

Would George Bailey have witnessed the same far-reaching impact from his life if he had lived only for his work? Would he have helped so many people in so many diverse ways if he had allowed himself to be held prisoner in his own office? If he had focused narrowly on maximizing profits rather than on helping people through his Building and Loan business, would his impact have been more like that of his nemesis, Mr. Potter, who lived only for his own selfish aggrandizement? George Bailey's wonderful life, like that of any of us, was the product of time spent nurturing many different fields of endeavor, including his family, his friends, and his community. And while he frequently denied himself most of his more grandiose fantasies, such as to become a world traveler, along the way to helping others he found the time to make himself a better and "richer" person too.

The only way to ensure you have sufficient time for such life-enriching experiences is to make appointments with yourself. And make them regularly and often if you want to build "a wonderful life" from the clutter of pieces lying all around you. If you want to have lunch with your spouse or get involved with a church or attend your child's baseball game or play handball or do volunteer work, make an appointment on your schedule. Then, treat it as if it were as important as any other appointment, because it is. Do not consider it a tentative throw-away, to be hastily discarded if any other "more important" demand on your time comes up. Protect that time from other activities just as you would an appointment to meet with your boss's boss's boss.

One such appointment with yourself should be regular, frequent, aerobic exercise. Fitness is an important part of being a productive, active human being. It is most emphatically not a luxury. Do not feel guilty or apologize for taking the time to exercise. You will be better able to perform your duties, with improved stamina and with fewer sick days, if you are in good physical condition. You will be able to work and play harder and longer and at a greater energy level. Moreover, exercise improves your mental outlook and gives you a chance to "clear your head." Many useful ideas and solutions to problems come to people while they are jogging, walking, bicycling, swimming, or engaging in other stimulating exercise.

Keep your exercise appointments with yourself. Breaking them would be costly to you, both personally and professionally. Most important are the long-term effects of exercise or the lack thereof. As you get older, you will either reap the benefits of regular exercise or pay for your neglect of your body with poor health and diminished quality and/or quantity of life.

Breaks are a valuable time tactic. If you try to sit at your desk hour after hour, slogging through your work, eventually you will suffer a fall-off in effectiveness and productivity. In addition to your regular exercise appointments, take a short walk or stretch several times during the day. Even a five-minute walk or a few stretching exercises will give your mind and body welcome relief and enable you to remain at a high level of effectiveness for a prolonged period. You may think you are impressing somebody by remaining at your desk for hour after hour, as though you were Ben Hur chained to his oars in the bowels of a Roman war ship, but all you are really accomplishing is a real-life demonstration of the law of diminishing returns.

Please do not fall into the sometimes-tempting trap of robbing Peter to pay Paul, or, more precisely, robbing yourself of sleep to pay the time collectors. Trying to make more time for other things by cutting back on your sleep is, at best, a marginally effective short-term desperation measure to be reserved for the most extraordinary emergencies.

You should know from experience about how much sleep your body and mind require in order to restore your faculties sufficiently for the next day's challenges and opportunities. You have noticed that when you get less than a certain amount of sleep there are more or less adverse consequences. You are probably more irritable, more error-prone, more erratic in your decision-making, and more likely to have an injury-causing accident. You are also probably less able to concentrate, less creative, less resistant to getting sick, and less energetic. Your stamina is diminished. You are running on vapor. You may be shortening your life itself through prolonged sleep deficits. You are literally living on borrowed time.

Unless you are one of the rare individuals who currently is getting more sleep than is needed, steer clear of the sleep deprivation school of time management. No one can live on borrowed time for very long without paying it all back with a hefty rate of interest. In fact, it may be that you need more sleep than you have been allowing yourself. Take a hard look at your needs, and be honest with yourself. You may well discover that budgeting a bit more slumber into your schedule more than pays for itself in enhanced productivity, creativity, and overall quality of life during those hours when you are awake.

You need not necessarily get all of your sleep in one session. Some people, such as Thomas Edison, have found that short naps can have wonderful restorative powers and can enable them to function very well with less sleep at night. If possible, try a brief siesta and see whether this is something that could work for you. You may not be another Edison, but you may be a better and more inventive version of yourself as a result. A nap just long enough to revitalize you without making you sluggish can be a very intelligent way of making more time for yourself by taking a break.

Longer breaks, in the form of vacations, are also essential to your well-being and productivity. Vacations are not a waste of time. You are doing no one any favors by failing to use your annual allotment of vacation time. By getting out of your usual environment and routine, you will rejuvenate your spirits and learn significant lessons about yourself and about life. Vacations are a vital ingredient in your personal health and the health of your interpersonal relationships. You will form and strengthen bonds with other people during these extended breaks that otherwise would wither away through lack of care. And the memories you make during your vacations will, in retrospect, much more likely fit the description of "a wonderful life" than those forged through an extra couple of weeks each year with your nose firmly pressed to the ever-whirling grindstone.

A Passport to Brigadoon

If you have never seen the Broadway musical play *Brigadoon* or the motion picture based on it, you are missing something special. This great Lerner-and-Loewe musical brings a vital message along with its gorgeous songs and captivating story.

Brigadoon is a little Scottish village than appears for only one day every one hundred years. After this one day is over, everyone in Brigadoon falls asleep for an entire century, and the entire place vanishes from sight for anyone outside the village in the "real world." But as one visitor from the United States learned when he stumbled upon Brigadoon during that once-in-a-century day, there is one way an outsider can hold onto the vision and prevent it from disappearing at the end of the day. Love is the key to that unseen door.

If you love someone enough, you can remain in Brigadoon. The setting of the sun will not cause everything to fade from view but instead will mark the beginning of another phase of life. Eventually, the sun will rise again and everyone around you will live once more.

The American visitor fell in love with a woman from the village and by the conclusion of the story won his spot in the wondrous place. The final line of the play reads "When you love someone enough, anything is possible...even miracles!"

It seems that the older we become, the faster time sweeps past us. As they say in Brigadoon, "Soon now, 'tis the end of our day." Where does our life go? The future, which once seemed so limitless, suddenly and frighteningly has an end in sight. But, wait! Our lives cannot end! We have so many things left to do!

Exactly. We all have so many more things to do than we ever could fit into one lifetime. Our lives, in the context of the vastness of the time lines of human history, are much like the one day of Brigadoon. . .so wonderful and so soon gone.

Can we somehow create more time? Can we get a passport for Brigadoon that will enable us to stay, at least, a little while longer? In a very real sense, the answer to both of these questions is yes. That is the reason this chapter was written. If we follow some of the principles we have been discussing, we may "make" time for the many worthwhile pursuits of life by "taking" time from factors that had caused it to be unwisely spent.

If we love deeply enough, we can make this miracle happen. If we love the people and things in life that make living much more than merely existing and if we love someone or some principle more than we love ourselves, we can find the passport to Brigadoon. This is the type of love it takes to make us resolve to be better than we are and to change our ways.

Motivated by love, we can restructure our way of living, putting aside some things and taking up others. Our lives may become less stressful as a result. And if we devote some of that newfound time to healthy activities such as exercise, we may actually prolong our lives as well. Even one additional day is of inestimable value to a person who longs to remain a bit longer but is facing the door of death.

To return again to the story of Ebenezer Scrooge, it took the personal intervention of multiple supernatural beings to persuade him that Bob Cratchit was not being slovenly for wanting "the whole day off" on Christmas. It required a face-to-face confrontation with "Death" itself to bring him to understand that his own material wealth, no matter how vast, would not substitute for a poverty of love. For some of us, unscheduled appointments with three or four ghosts prob-

ably would not suffice to get us to take some time off, so sure
are we that it is only our constant efforts that keep the world
spinning on its axis. Meanwhile, the sands in our hourglass
continue to slip, irretrievable, away from us, relentlessly and
unstoppably, every second of every minute of every day.

This is a simple but elusive truth. Time, once spent, can
never be recouped. It can slip away so easily. As songwriter
and co-author of this book, John C. Kunich wrote in, "Time
Machine."

> When I was younger, I dreamed of a time
> machine,
> To take me ahead, to an age I'd never seen.
> I dreamed of a time machine.
>
> I couldn't wait to learn how to drive,
> I couldn't wait for my birthdays to arrive,
> I couldn't wait till I'd move away,
> I couldn't wait till "Someday."
>
> Time machine, I dreamed of a time machine,
> To speed me ahead,
> To the future, where I should be,
> I dreamed of a time machine.
>
> Now that I'm older, I dream of a time
> machine,
> To bring me back home, to an age that's
> evergreen,
> I dream of a time machine.
>
> I can recall a bright springtime day,
> I can recall all I had to do was play,
> I can recall my life, new and clean,
> Before I tore through it on my time machine.

Time machine, I dream of a time machine,
To give back the years,
And a second chance to be me,
I dream of a time machine.

The time management techniques outlined in this chapter are not intended to turn people into robots, hard-wired to do nothing but work, with cold, bloodless persistence and efficiency. In fact, our purpose is quite the opposite. By carefully evaluating what truly matters most to us and deciding what we want most to achieve in all aspects of our lives–personal, social, familial, professional–we can then use these methods to minimize waste and maximize the amount of time we have available to live our lives in all their multifaceted diversity.

The effect of such self-study can be dramatically transformational. Like Scrooge on Christmas morning after the last ghost had departed, we may find ourselves profoundly grateful that no matter what mistakes we have made before we are still alive. We still have some time left. We can change the way we live our lives. We can change the way we spend our precious grains of sand, the quicksand of time. We can tarry in Brigadoon a little longer.

Discussion Questions and Ideas

- How many of the following methods do you currently use to keep track of things you need to do?
  a) Paper lists
  b) Scraps of paper
  c) Post-it type notes
  d) Palm Pilot
  e) Wall calendar
  f) Desk calendar

g) Project management software
h) Paper notebook or organizer
i) Mental notes to yourself
j) Asking others to remind you
k) Project management chalkboard
l) Other

- To what extent do you find it difficult to avoid either duplication or omission of such reminders? Why?

- What are some examples of time-consuming activities in your life that are urgent but not important? Is there a way you can eliminate them?

- What are some examples of activities in your life that you consider important but not urgent? Do you usually find time to do them? If so, how? If not, why not?

- Are there any time-thieves in your current workplace? How do they interact with you? How much of your time do they waste per week, on average? What can you do to safeguard more of your time from them?

- Are there any projects you have been meaning to tackle, but have put off because of lack of time? Is there a way you can begin at least one of these projects this week?

- What do you consider the most important five goals in your life? What do you do, specifically, each week in furtherance of each of these goals?

- What do you consider the least productive, least important activity to which you now devote at least one hour per week? Why do you engage in this activity? What can you do to reduce or eliminate the time you spend on it?

- Write your own obituary as you would like it to read. For what do you want to be remembered by your family, your friends, and the world? How much time are you devoting each week to making these a reality?

- Are there any skills you currently lack that could make you more efficient and more productive? Some possible examples:
  a) Typing
  b) Using e-mail
  c) Using word processors
  d) Computer-aided project management
  e) Spreadsheets
  f) Databases
  g) Using Palm Pilot

Bibliography and Recommended Reading

Griessman, Eugene B. *Time Tactics of Very Successful People*. New York: McGraw-Hill Professional Publishing, 1994.

Covey, Stephen R. *First Things First: to Live, to Love, to Learn, to Leave a Legacy.* New York: Simon and Schuster, 1996.

Blanchard, Kenneth H. *The One-Minute Manager Meets the Monkey*. New York: William Morrow & Co., 1989.

APPENDIX A
A Five-minute Survival Kit for Emergencies

Listed below are selected concepts, skills, and actions a leader should consider when they first "get the call" to take a leadership position.

Strategic-Level Leadership

- Establish an effective working relationship with your subordinates and peers.

- Envision the future and repeatedly convey your vision to a wide audience. Create a clear mission and values centered vision. Continually renew and refresh its execution.

- Be a persuader with exceptional moral courage and a broad-range sense of responsibility and discipline.

- Communicate effectively. In distance situations, effective communication requires: careful attention to listening, presenting your thoughts and ideas as clearly as possible, and focusing on conveying positive and constructive mission intent.

- Read widely, if not deeply, from history and give careful attention to hot button issues.

- Create an environment of accomplishment, excitement, and trust. Reward improvements and celebrate results by acknowledging people and

accomplishments. Earn the loyalty of your subordinates and select outstanding personnel for
promotion and awards.

- Prize ability (i.e., competence), willingness (i.e.,
motivation), and the people who demonstrate
those traits. Build teams maximizing these qualities.

- Give top priority to building organizations that
effectively work together to accomplish broad
organizational objectives.

- Realize you function in an uncertain environment, facing highly complex problems often im-
pacted by people, events, and organizations outside your organization. Understand these forces
and work within them.

Organizational-level Leadership

- Understand an organization is an "open social
system" i.e., all aspects of an organization are interrelated.

- Be passionately focused on understanding the
character, scope, nature, and purpose of the organization you lead.

- Insist on excellence at every level and be intoler-
ant of unnecessary rules and regulations that stifle
and suppress initiative and creativity. Remember
the best organizational leaders understand leadership is the liberating of talent.

- Always search for and apply the best ideas regardless of their source.

- Demonstrate an infectious enthusiasm for perspectives and skills requiring highly developed competency, character, steadfastness, and boldness to achieve the mission.

- Establish the organizational structure to focus efforts. Plan and organize activities necessary to get results. Motivate and influence the organization to accomplish the mission.

- Always lead with unyielding integrity and strong personal devotion to the organization you serve.

- Understand good organizations are adaptive, cohesive, and resilient.

- Do not become indispensable. Organizations need indispensable functions not indispensable people.

- Give top attention to building organizations from teams.

Direct-level Leadership

- Value direct face-to-face leadership and leader visibility within an organization.

- Be close enough to operations to see up front how things work, how things do not work, and how to address problems.

- Good leadership involves responsibility to the

interests of the group. This can mean some people will be angry at your actions and decisions. Always do what is right. Be guided by your instincts and core values.

- Keep commitments, admit mistakes, keep confidences, and demonstrate respect for all members and their opinions. They have value.

- Be certain to model the behavior expected of all members.

- Always take the initiative to make things better.

- Be active in helping others diagnose and solve problems.

- Assert yourself in helping people to constructively move from conflict to collaboration.

- Seek out opportunities to recognize members' contributions to a results-oriented environment.

- Always, with unyielding integrity, build teams from individuals.

Personal-level Leadership

- Smoke out those of low integrity; be goal oriented, and lead by example.

- Link core values to daily activities.

- Emphasize the need to reach or exceed expectations for performance and results.

- Continually stress the need for goal-directed self-discipline in completing daily work.

- Ensure all personnel understand how their contributions impact others and the unit as a whole.

- Help all personnel understand their roles and responsibilities and how they are linked to team building.

- Actively seek to build teamwork and collaboration across groups and functions. Establish mutual involvement in situations crossing organizational boundaries.

- Be alert to helping personnel identify opportunities for improvement in mission taskings and processes impacting the overall mission.

- Vigorously challenge assumptions inhibiting progress toward mission achievement.

- Carefully clarify the rationale and intent of goals and supporting objectives.

APPENDIX B
Survival Kit for Your Pocket

- Be Active
- Stay in Touch
- Remember Your Heroes' Examples
- Provide Feedback To Feed the Hands That Back You
- Mentor for All It's Worth
- Make Time Management First, Not Last
- Never Violate Legal or Ethical Principles
- Learn from Your Mistakes
- Have a Value System
- Know How to Communicate
- Know Your Job
- Know Your Boss's Job
- Make Your Boss's Job Easier
- Have Fun
- Be a Visionary
- Be Visible
- Lead by Example
- Be a Good Listener
- Take Care of Your Subordinates First
- Praise in Public/Discipline in Private
- Share Your Knowledge
- Stand Up for Your People
- Be Aware of What Your People Are Doing
- Be a Risk Taker/Innovator
- Be Compassionate
- Don't Make Yourself Indispensable